MAKING THE CASE

THE NO-NONSENSE GUIDE TO WRITING
THE PERFECT CASE STATEMENT

JEROLD PANAS

*"Your draft of the Case Statement has my basic thrust. Have it
fleshed out, pretty'd-up, fussed over, given a shot of pizzaz,
minimize the cost of the project, make the memorial opportunities
sexier, shorten the headlines but add a lot more sizzle, get more
exciting photos, cut the length, give me more details, find more
inspiring quotations, get Board approval, and have it back
tomorrow morning in final form."*

First printed November 2003

10 9 8 7 6 5 4 3 2 1

Printed in the United States of America

Library of Congress Catalog Card Number: 2003112737

ISBN: 0-9746084-0-8

Copies of this book are available from the publisher at discount when purchased in quantity for boards of directors or staff.

INSTITUTIONS PRESS

500 North Michigan Avenue, 20th Floor
Chicago, Illinois 60611
(800) 234-7777 | Fax (312) 222-9411

LET'S GO

I always had the idea that as I got older, I'd get frightfully clever. I'd get awfully learned. I'd get jolly sage. I thought people would come to me for advice, seek my wisdom, sit at my feet for some wonderful pearls of learning. But nobody ever comes to me for anything. I'm beginning to think I don't know a bloody thing. I think I'll write a book.

– Rex Harrison

To all who feel the yet unfulfilled itch to write, and to all who are about to begin a Case Statement, and to all others who have written a goodly share of Cases— this book is dedicated to you. To all of you.

But especially for those who haven't yet started, I urge you to sit down and begin. Just start writing.

When General Eisenhower launched the D-Day invasion, his instructions were: "Okay, let's go."

So go ahead. Just start writing. If I can do it, you can too. Okay, let's go...

"Everyday I begin my writing with the same odd feeling, that I am on trial for my life and will probably not be acquitted."

– Franz Kafka

TABLE OF CONTENTS

**Everything you need to know about
Writing a Case Statement**

1

DANCE WITH
THE BEARS

*"An author is allowed to say: This and that are so, you must
believe me. And an author is expected to say: My truth is the only
truth that matters— my truth. And if you don't like it,
you can lump it."*

– W. Somerset Maugham

I'M NOT A WRITER. That's what makes me such a good choice
to write about Case Statements.

I'll explain.

I do not earn my bread and board by writing. I am not a professional writer. But I love to write. Long ago I found in myself
cacoethia scribendi— the urge to scribble.

Sure, I've written Case Statements. Plenty. I suppose dozens
and dozens. And I've edited…well, I'll bet it's close to a thousand.
That's not an exaggeration.

But here's what is important. I'm the one who actually has to
use a Case Statement. I review them with leaders when I conduct a
feasibility study and I use them for calling on prospects for gifts.

In a sense, as they say, I walk the talk.

I'm not going to give you much philosophy in these chapters. The discourse here is one of joy and motivation. My mother would have liked it.

This book is all about inspiring men and women to do great things for your cause. Nuts and bolts.

This much I know: A person is not willing to creep when they feel the impulse to soar. I want to help you give your readers wings.

Even just "average" writing is plenty tough. "There is nothing to writing," said the great sports columnist Red Smith. "All you do is sit down and open up a vein."

An author comes to that frightful jumping-off place. It is that dark and terrifying moment when she must simply put down on paper that miraculous strike of lightning— the opening sentence. You know the feeling.

"It's intimidating, enough to freeze great minds and pure hearts into permanent silence," says John Updike. "Writing is terrible work— the leap onto blank paper, the precarious linkage of one sentence to the next. Just beginning, that demon first word, is a terrifying experience."

An effective Case Statement grabs a person and never lets go. It inspires and motivates the reader to go from their mind to their heart to their purse. That's what it must do. Flaubert said he wanted the writing to be so exciting you could, "bang out tunes that could make bears dance."

This book is all about writing a Case Statement. We are all seekers and explorers in this journey. The French say: *Tous les*

Beaux Esprits se Rencontrent. Roughly translated, it means beautiful spirits seek each other out.

I guide you through each step. You will find I sometimes do not agree with what others have written about Case Statements. That's because most articles and books on Case Statements are written by writers, not by users.

I feel like the Apostle Paul when he wrote to the Galatians: "What I write is the plain truth." What I write in this book, you can count on.

This book will be particularly helpful to those who have never before written a Case Statement. It will be beneficial, also, to experienced professional writers who haven't yet undertaken an actual Case Statement. (Case Statements are different.) It will even help those who have written only a few. It should be fun for the latter group, and confirming.

Even where it may disagree with what you have been doing or what you've been taught, it will be like the *Broccoli Syndrome:* You know it's good for you even though you don't like it.

I want you to write in this book. Scrawl all over it. Write in the margins, circle, use a highlighter. Take possession.

The effective Case Statement has the distinctive character and near finality of a beautiful Bach cantata. It begins by breaking the silence and ends by returning the silence, and leaves everything in between completely resolved. You and I are going to make beautiful music together.

"I'm willing to give to you if I'm properly motivated by a Case Statement that has high dramatic and emotional impact."

2

REACH FOR THE STARS

Abbott is the author of "Babies." Not long ago, he sent 500 copies of the book to a charity for one of their auctions. A member of the committee decided to read the book— and felt it was not at all appropriate for their institution. The board decided to return the 500 books to Abbott.

He was furious, really upset. Abbott put all 500 books in his van, returned to the site of the auction, and burned the books in front of those in attendance.

The blaze spread. Soon, four houses were on fire. When the fire department finally arrived, Abbot jumped in his van and gunned the motor. Before he got away, someone heard him say: "It's tough being a writer nowadays."

I AM SITTING IN THE OFFICE of Bonnie McElveen-Hunter. On her couch is a quotation embroidered on a pillow: *Life is Short, Hell is Hot, and the Stakes are High.*

Now that's what I call a command to action.

If you've flown USAir, United, or Delta, you know Bonnie because her firm prepares those wonderful in-flight magazines you love to thumb through. Now that you know her better, you'll be pleased to learn that on top of all of her other achievements, she's been appointed United States Ambassador to Finland.

She is a generous donor and one of the most effective solicitors I've ever worked with. I spoke to someone Bonnie had just called on for a gift. She asked Harriet for a million dollars. (She gave it!) Afterwards, Harriet said to me: "How could anyone ever say *no* to Bonnie."

Bonnie and I get to talking about Case Statements. "I want writing that grabs the reader by the throat and never lets go." That's what Bonnie tells me.

She isn't talking about fluff or hyperbole. That's repugnant. Readers can smell that stuff a mile away.

But you do want passion and energy. Conviction and zeal. You want every word, as St. Bernard of Clairvaux once observed, to be so forceful a blow that it smites the devil.

John Ruskin said: "If the writing touches the reader, there is a sudden sense that the stars had been blown out of the sky." Your job is to reach for the stars and blow them out of the sky.

But you must know your market and your giving constituency. I've learned my lesson in this regard, but it's taken a long time.

We recently completed a Case Statement for a seminary in the southwest. The manuscript was approved by the president and several members of the board. It didn't have quite the action of the chariot scene from *Ben Hur* (that would not have been a fair representation of this seminary), but it did have a certain pace and passion.

Then we send it for review to the person who is very likely their largest potential donor to the campaign. (A superb cultivation move.)

She e-mails me: "This is the worst Case Statement I've ever read, and I've read a lot of them. It's terrible. You should be embarrassed. I want you to write it again and if you don't get it right this time, I'll do it myself. I don't want an adjective, I don't want an adverb. Just straight writing."

"The old simple words are the best," Hemingway said. But I don't think this is what he had in mind.

I don't have to go to a seminar on *How to Write a Case Statement* to know I am in serious trouble. It is like being between a dog and the lamppost. You know that feeling.

My first reaction is to defend the Case Statement. I feel like the old high school Latin teacher protecting the punch bowl at the Prom.

But, of course, I realize we have to make serious changes. In fact, we start all over from scratch. That's almost always easier than trying to do a major revision. Attempting a sizable reworking of a manuscript is tantamount to reconstructing a spider's web.

A new draft is prepared for the Seminary. No adjectives, no adverbs. Not one. I think it gives the feeling of the pendulous motion of a leaf falling through still air. It reads like the social notes in a Methodist Church newsletter.

We submit the new draft to our prospective donor. She loves it. Loves it! We then send it to the president and several members of the board. They love it. Somewhere in the background I hear the theme from Rocky.

The lesson is: Know your market. Hundreds of copies of the Case will be distributed. Perhaps thousands. But remember you are pulling out all the stops for an audience of one.

The St. Louis Children's Hospital is considered one of the five most outstanding in the country. Some of their specialties and sub-specialties are regarded as the world's best. They are premier in every way— except, alas, for their record of fundraising.

I am finishing a meeting with the Board of Trustees, admonishing them for not raising the funds they deserve. (They have now turned that completely around with a new vice president who is extremely effective and a new CEO who likes to ask for gifts.)

I say to the Board they are leaving money on the table. I tell them it's because they really don't know why they need to raise funds and don't know how the funds will be used.

The moment is suddenly flooded with silence. A thundering quiet. It is a World Series silence. You know, the sort of hush when the Visiting Team has scored eight runs in the first inning.

No one speaks. They are as tight-lipped as a card playing Lutheran on a losing streak. I want to do hand puppets or perhaps recite Gertrude Stein. It's what John Steinbeck described as, "the urge to be someplace else."

The chair finally speaks. "You know, Jerry. You're absolutely right. We don't know what we want to raise money for." Everyone on the Board nods in agreement.

Keep this in mind.

We almost always think of a Case Statement as an absolutely

essential tool in preparing for a capital campaign. And it is. It is the *mother ship* of all other material.

But note this. The Case Statement is just as important for ongoing, annual giving. Just as important for planned giving. And for corporate gifts. And foundation grants.

If you are interested in raising funds, your institution needs a current Case Statement. Period! If money is important to you, you need a Case Statement.

When you have the Case, it should be reviewed, assessed, and revised (if necessary) on a regular basis. It is your basic document— that which gives spirit, vitality, and purpose to all you do. It is your *Institutional Credo.*

The Case explains why you are worthy of voluntary effort and financial support. It defines who benefits and why your organization is uniquely positioned to provide the services and use the funds effectively.

Here's the crucial question your Case must answer: "Why do these folks deserve my support?" That's the nub of it. Your readers will want to be certain your organization is a wise place to invest their money. Be certain you explain what the dividends will be.

As the prospect reads the Case, she will be thinking: "Among my philanthropic interests, how can I determine where to place your organization?" You'd better provide the right answer.

"What will my gift accomplish?" That's what the reader wants to know. "And why your organization?" The prospect wants assurance the gift will have powerful influence on those touched by your service today— and in the future.

Let's start here: People don't want to give money away. That's not the motivation.

They want to invest in a bold and heroic cause. They want their funds used to change lives or save lives. You want them to know that by giving, they have the power to make great things happen.

It's their money. It's their decision. They want to see the impact.

Don't ask for their money. Go for their heart. Ask for their investment to change lives or save lives.

If you capture their soul and spirit, you succeed in what John D. Rockefeller called: "The difficult art of giving."

3

ONE SUIT DOESN'T FIT ALL

"In my own case, there are days when the result is so bad that no fewer than six or seven revisions are required. However, when I'm greatly inspired only five revisions are necessary before even my meanest critics concede: 'Galbraith has that wonderful spark of spontaneity.'"

– John Kenneth Galbraith

FOR YEARS I'VE PREPARED and furnished clients with Case Statements. Some were downright dazzling. (Well, yes...and some less than that.)

But I am embarrassed. And I would not care to admit this to anybody but you. It is only in the past few years it occurred to me that the same Case Statement, no matter how brilliant, cannot be effective with all constituencies of an organization.

Think about it. It makes sense.

Take a hospital, for instance. The Case Statement you prepare for former patients does not necessarily have the same importance and impact on the medical staff. And take, for another example, the attitude of former donors and the concerns of the nursing staff. They do not react the same way nor have the same imperatives.

Here's a sample of the various constituencies of a typical hospital. I've listed eleven distinct groups. There may be more. There is overlapping, of course. But each has its own interests, its own characteristics, its own degrees of provincialism.

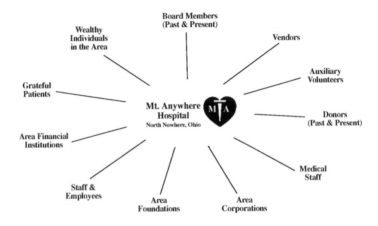

The typical college is a bit different.

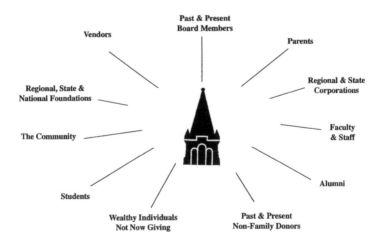

It's like buying clothes. One suit doesn't fit all.

Think for a moment about the large and beautiful mirror-speckled sphere on the ceiling above the dance floor at the prom. It sends out spangles of light, beaming fragmentary particles at different dancers. That's what your Case should be doing with your different constituencies.

One very good Case may do the over-arching job for several of your constituencies. But for some special groups, you are going to want a Case that has a riveting and distinctive focus on them specifically.

Keep in mind, one suit doesn't fit all.

No matter how many separate Case Statements you end up with, there are seven ways a Statement is used.

1. It assures and secures agreement, understanding, and commitment among your primary leaders and Board members. There can be no question there is total dedication to the cause and a precise understanding of the institution's objectives and long-range goals.

   Everyone must agree. This is more difficult than it may appear. On the part of the Board, they sign-off with faith and courage, wisdom and spirit.

2. It provides a direction and a defined strategy for how to present your vision and the urgency to your primary constituencies most effectively and dramatically. It becomes an expert witness for your mission.

3. The Case informs leaders and workers of your program and your audacious dreams. It demonstrates and substantiates how the success of the endeavor will work to the immense and unending benefit of those you serve.

You need not be modest here. I give you permission to state your dreams with near the wild abandonment and giddiness of a sailor on leave. The words leap from the reader's brain, then take over his heart.

4. The effective Case enlists friends and new leaders to your cause, in sufficient numbers and at the proper level to win the effort. It is effective at this because the Statement defines the purpose of the proposed program and shapes the destiny of the organization.

5. It is an early working document and cultivation piece for prospective major donors. I love using it this way.

I let major donors know it is still in draft form, a work in progress— but I want them to be among the first to review it and suggest changes. It's a *Gotcha*. Used this way, it is wonderfully engaging in a captivating way.

6. It is a document that helps others endorse and share your vision. They accept a greater and ever-expanding responsibility of identifying with your invincible mission and dreams. Robert Frost called it that immense energy of life which sparks a fire.

It is nothing less than the soul and spirit reaching toward infinity. Readers share your vision with great courage and high-wire impudence.

7. Nothing happens until you first describe the dream. Then the Case becomes the source book and guide for the writing of subsequent publications, articles, foundation proposals, and video presentations.

The Case provides the pursuit of the possible. It transforms the mission into dreams, and the dreams into results.

Did you notice? I didn't once mention money in the list I just gave you.

What? Not mention money in the Case?

I want you to refocus your eyes and your thinking. Imagine a different way of seeing things. Look at a pair of stairs, for instance. Are the stairs going up or down?

Oh, sure. At some point in the Case, you have to talk about how much the dream is going to cost. A Case Statement is, after all, a vision with dollar signs after it.

But keep in mind that neither the focus nor the objective of philanthropy is about money.

Do you and I see things the same? We have to get together and compare notes to make absolutely sure. But I think we do.

The shelf life of a tepid Case Statement is somewhere between milk and yogurt. You want a Case that is read and devoured. An unending feast of inspiration.

Your Case is about soaring aspirations. It is often about new ideas in confrontation with the old. There will be some who find this uncomfortable. Your job is to make the risk challenging, exciting, and fulfilling.

You are the writer. You are the phrase spinner and image weaver, a wordsmith of uncompromising power and force.

You define the objectives. You inspire confidence, dispel questions, propel desired actions. You light the candles.

These bold plans you present will take a certain daring for some of your readers. For them, it will be like jumping off a steep cliff. Your job is to build their wings for the way down.

4

WONDROUS MIRACLES

*"A man who knows not how to write may think this is no great feat.
But only try to do it yourself and you will learn how arduous is the
writer's task. It dims your eyes, makes your back ache, and knits your
chest and belly together— it is a terrible ordeal for the human body.
So, gentle reader, turn these pages carefully and keep your
fingers far from the text."*

– Prior Robert Alden, C1300 AD

I JUST FINISHED TALKING with Virginia Piper about a new Science Building for Xavier High School in Phoenix. Virginia was one of the most memorable and most generous persons I have ever known. She had the kind of charm and a smile that could give you hope in February.

Virginia is another and a better story, but for another day. She is now in heaven helping angels with wondrous miracles and celestial deeds.

I'm in Virginia's living room. I discover that the proposed Science Building for Xavier is of some interest to her. But only of modest consequence. It's really the mission of the School that is particularly fascinating to her— the fact that it is all girls, and the emphasis on rigorous scholarship. She loves the focus on developing leadership in young women.

No one from the School has ever called on her before. I can tell she is mildly interested in the Science Building…but head-over-heels excited about the School.

"Do you have something to leave that I can read?"

(It's only a matter of personal style, but I don't like trotting out printed material until after I've made the presentation. Sometimes I don't even do that. Most often, I prefer putting it in the mail for the prospect to read along with a letter thanking them for the visit. It reinforces the visit and the presentation.)

I hand Virginia the Case Statement. I wouldn't typically do that but she asks for it, and it seems appropriate.

The Case is called, *The 7th Hour.* I won't bother you now with the rationale for the title, but it does have striking significance to the School.

(As a matter of fact, I thought the title was rather intriguing. It answers the implacable job of a title: To get the reader into the material. It is the thread throughout the document that ties everything to everything— and ties all of it into a neat package at the end.)

"May I take a moment to read it now?"

(I consider that an excellent augury. I'm lighting Holy Candles. If she was so-so about the project, she could simply have asked me to leave it behind, and usher me out the door.)

An extraordinary thing happens. I see a keenness glowing within her like the pilot being turned up on a gas stove.

The Case somehow gets a headlock on her she can't break. She loves it. She reads some passages out loud to me. I feel like a lucky Jonah who has just swallowed my whale.

(I take a moment of personal privilege and pardonable pride. This happens to be a Case Statement I wrote. The congregation will please rise.)

Virginia excuses herself. She goes into the little study off the living room. When she comes back, she hands me a check.

I peek at it, trying not to be too obvious. Good grief! It's a check for $50,000.

"I'm so impressed with the story of Xavier, I want to be a part of the program."

I hand the check back. (You wonder why. I'll explain. We were actually hoping to ask for a larger gift on the next visit. Much larger. If I take the $50,000 check, it makes it very difficult to ask for the larger gift.)

She insists I take it. I finally decide to accept it. I ask for a new time we can plan on another visit.

A second visit is made, this time with Sister Joan, the Head of the School. It is very successful.

You will be pleased to know that the new Science Building at Xavier is called, The Virginia Piper Science Center.

I find no matter how dazzling the oral presentation, you must be able to describe in writing the project and its need. You must also be able to substantiate why your institution is uniquely positioned to fulfill the program you propose.

The Case Statement is not a campaign folder, although ultimately it will very likely be the basis of the major brochure. It isn't mailed with a request for a gift. It is not meant to be a piece for direct response mailings. It is too important for that.

The Case Statement is the mother of all your materials.

It is often left behind after the presentation for a gift. It could very well be the hammer that helps nail the gift in place.

Be creative with the use of the Case Statement. Make it work for you. Lately, I've been sending it in advance of a call to my top prospects. Try it. I find it immensely effective.

Here's what I do. I mark it with a big red rubber stamp that says **DRAFT.** It is sent prior to the visit. The letter that accompanies it reads something like:

> *I am so pleased we are going to be able to get together. Before our visit, I would like you to take a few minutes to read about this new program. I think you're going to find it very exciting.*
>
> *Please feel free to make notes on your copy of the material. The piece isn't quite final yet. I do want to get your reaction to the program. Mark your copy up or circle any areas that you may wish to discuss when we are together.*

This is what I find. To my absolute delight. When my top prospects are asked to read the DRAFT, with a request to help with the story— they actually will read it. And mark it up.

At St. Louis Children's Hospital, Jim Miller sent a red ink pen with the Case. He asked potential donors to mark it up. And they did. (It's such a good idea, I'm going to claim it was mine.)

But be prepared. I've had some badly marked up. I feel the same pain that must have befallen Albert Payson Terune, the author of *Lassie,* who had to be taken to the Emergency Room, when he was bitten by a collie.

I love having prospects make notes about the copy and offer suggestions. All of a sudden it becomes their Case Statement, not the institution's. When they tell me how they would like to improve it, I consider that a *Gotcha.*

The Case Statement is the centerpiece of your fundraising effort. It is the document from which all other components of the project emulate.

I like to use it with my top prospects, let's say for the key one hundred who have the potential for making or influencing the largest gifts. These one hundred will likely contribute 80% or so of what you raise.

With donors who have the very largest potential, I much prefer using a Case Statement that's modest in appearance rather than an expensive campaign brochure. It is unadorned, although tastefully assembled. It gives the appearance of a low cost, no-nonsense explanation of what the program is all about.

(As you know, your major donors don't want you spending a lot on 4-color, die cut, embossed material. The inexpensively produced Case fits the bill perfectly.)

The Case Statement is just as important for your volunteers. It will help them understand the program.

There are a number of components to the Case Statement. But never mind that for now. I describe these in the next few chapters.

Ultimately, the Case is an irresistible roster of all the substantiated reasons a person should support your mighty cause. It is what John Gardner so perfectly called, "the presentation of your noble and vivid dream."

5

WHY SHOULD I INVEST?

"Most of the time I do nothing. I waste most of my time in daydreaming, in drawing faces on pieces of paper. I do it by the hour before I can finally begin my day of writing."

– Saul Bellow

I AM TALKING WITH MARK, a highly successful venture capitalist. His wife is with us. We're discussing the independent school their youngster goes to in a *katish* suburb of Boston.

The family loves the School. "It has changed our son's life," he says. She adds: "It is the greatest thing that has ever happened to our family. Everything about it is wonderful."

"But this Prospectus is terrible." That's Mark talking.

(You've probably guessed this isn't a propitious start! Mark's words become the fingernails on my chalkboard.)

"The truth is, if this was a business, I wouldn't buy it. Wouldn't even consider it." That's Mark again. (Being a venture capitalist, he thinks of the Case as being a Prospectus for a business— which in a sense it is.)

I feel a little like Walt Whitman, wondering "how I can possibly uncrumble this much-crumbled thing."

By the way, this is not our Case Statement. Our writer made a first attempt at it but the school leadership felt we completely misunderstood the character of the School and hadn't captured its ethos.

The Review Committee really let me have it. It was too long, too wordy. They said it was tumid. (After the meeting, I had to look up the word but I was pretty certain it was not a positive comment.)

Well, you don't want to know all they said. It saddens me to admit all of this to you.

In a sense, we did not hear the message the Headmaster was trying to convey. A grievous offense for a writer. We did not hear the music of his mind and did not understand the spirit of his heart.

Then the Headmaster took it over and started writing from scratch. His is the document I am now sharing with the venture capitalist. I'm not saying whether it was better than our version or not. It certainly was different.

I think you should write your Case Statement the same way the popular crime novelist Elmore Leonard writes his mystery books. He is a literary genius who writes re-readable thrillers. When he was asked to explain why his books are so popular and so easy to read, Leonard answered: "It's simple. I just leave out the parts that readers skip."

Here's what is important. The Case is indeed much like a Prospectus. The potential investor (donor) wants to know: What are the irrefutable reasons I should invest (give) to this program? What dividends will I receive (what will the result be of my gift)? Why should I buy this company (give to your particular organization)? Is there a true market (is there a real need) for this service you're projecting?

You need to answer those questions in every Case you write. Each question.

Here's what the Case Statement should include. I'm actually listing these in the order I prefer engaging the item in the Case, bonding it to the section before and building on to the section that follows.

I use the theme (Title) throughout, from beginning to end. It is the thread that ties the entire piece into an enticing package. If you've chosen a powerful theme, it will really work for you. If you haven't chosen an exciting and emotional theme— start all over!

You may wish to inverse the order I give you in some way. Be my guest. Feel free to do whatever seems to make the flow easier, the piece much more spirited and readable, and the presentation more irresistible.

Eight elements are essential for your Case. They almost certainly will not be distinct sections in the material. But don't worry if they are. Some will overlap, some may be repeated, some will be in a different order.

It's okay. Just start writing. And make certain you cover each one.

1. **THE TITLE** The title develops the theme and tone for the Case Statement. Its inexorable job is to get the reader to turn to page one and begin reading the first few paragraphs.

2. **GRABBING THE READER** These are the first few introductory paragraphs that create an irresistible bridge into the material. If you lose the reader here, you'll never get him back. Often, a compelling quote in the early part of the Case works wonders.

3. **THE IRREFUTABLE CASE** Here you develop the need and

the urgency. It is important the Case becomes bigger and even more significant than the organization itself. (I explain this later.)

4. **YOUR UNIQUE POSITION** This describes how your institution is uncommonly positioned to meet the need head-on. This must burn itself into the minds and hearts of your readers.

5. **WAVING THE FLAG** Here you describe the strength of your organization, its mission, and history.

6. **REINFORCING THE URGENCY** This reminds the reader of how pressing the need is and that it must be dealt with immediately. The program cannot wait.

7. **MAKING IT HAPPEN** This describes what will be required financially to relieve the need. You achieve congruence with the reader.

8. **THE BENEDICTION** This provides the close and final blessing to the program. The theme, which has been used selectively and effectively throughout, is employed again at the end for emphasis.

I describe each one of these elements in more detail in chapters that follow. Don't worry about making each a separate segment in your writing. You probably shouldn't. Each will tend to intersect— like roads on their final journey to the successful reaching of your destination.

You're about ready to start. I want you to feel the impelling thrum. The Case Statement needs to be perceived as a tuning fork ready to vibrate when properly struck. It is, as the Psalmist says: "Giving voice as crashing cymbals."

6

WRITING THAT IGNITES A FIRE

*"I was a writing fool when I was eleven years old. And I've been
tapering off ever since. My professional writing life has been a long,
shameless exercise in avoidance.*

– E.B. White

S OME CASE STATEMENTS simply lie on a page, insipid and
unmoving. Dead on arrival.

What I look for is something majestic and inspirational,
vigorous and active— flapping like flags in high wind.

The most powerful weapon on earth is the human soul on fire.
Your Case bristles with excitement. The passion mounts and
accelerates, unable to stop— like the beating of a healthy heart.

I love the word, heartfully. Buried in that beautiful word is,
heart. Another word, *art.* Finally, one more word, *ear.* A good Case
Statement is the art of the listening heart. Edmund Wilson called it,
"a blaze of heartfelt ecstasy."

We wrote the Case Statement for Baylor University's $500
million campaign. It's important that top prospects have an

opportunity to review a draft of the Case Statement in order to test its appropriateness and motivational delivery. (I've mentioned this before— but repetition is good for the soul.)

Sending the Case in advance is also an extraordinary move in the cultivation process. It brings your top donors and volunteers one step closer into your institutional "hug."

Back to Baylor. It is an extraordinary institution. In their Case, we tried to match Baylor's Baptist fervor with words of glowing zeal and commitment. It was our dedication to ebullience.

One of their top prospects is a former English high school teacher. When she returned the draft of the Case Statement to me, it was lined in red like a crowded New Jersey roadmap. Sentences were struck, punctuation was changed, paragraphs were transposed.

She actually gave me a grade. She really did. It grieves me to tell you I received a D minus!

But I'm not worried about perfect English in my Case Statements. I don't want you to be either. Not everyone who reads your Case will be a former English teacher.

I want your material to grab the reader by the lapels and shake. I hope for an acute quake of ecstasy.

You want the Case Statement to be eminently readable, exciting, and inspiring. You're not trying to earn a high score on an SAT exam.

J'essaie de faire circular le sang á travers le marbre, the great sculpture Auguste Rodin said. "I try to make the blood circulate through the marble." That's what you hope to achieve— vital life circulating throughout the entirety of the manuscript.

Keep in mind, however— it's essential to know your institution and its giving constituencies. Remember: One Suit Doesn't Fit All.

We did the Case Statement for Fisk University. It's a wonderful school. It has one of the greatest art collections of any college in the country although that fact is unknown, even to many of the leaders in Nashville. Fisk is what is called an Historically Black College.

I prepare what I consider a heartfully written Case. It has passion, energy, and vision for the future. I am really delighted with the results. I present it to the president of Fisk and speak in a hushed and reverent voice— as a Cardinal might talk with the Holy Father.

He reads it. Then hands it back.

"You get a failing grade," President Smith tells me. "The grammar is terrible."

I tell him God does not much mind bad grammar. The President says that may be true, but He does not take any particular pleasure in it either.

"You don't understand, Jerry. I can live with the incomplete sentences, the contractions, and sentences ending with a preposition. I know what you are trying to achieve. But keep in mind how some of our prospects might perceive Fisk.

"I want them to think of us as a small Harvard right here in Nashville—with the highest quality education and the most scholarly faculty that exists anywhere. Our material has to reflect that."

The President is absolutely correct. I allotted my creativity and energy to the writing and gave scant thought to how the College would wish to be conveyed.

That's part of the secret. Know your institution and know your giving constituency. And be mindful of how the institution's ethos and character should be revealed.

You are the perception molder, the shape changer, the dream merchant. Your task is to bind the reader to an irresistible and irrefutable cause. You are saying: "My soul is going on a glorious trip. I want to take you with me." You want the reader to plunge into it, grasp it, explode!

7

RISK THE HOARY NO-NO'S

"I am about ready to begin my writing. My hands tremble. My head throbs. Every bone aches. My whole body shakes. The pain is so great I cannot think. My mind is a blank. I have stared at the paper in front of me for hours. Perhaps someone will call me for lunch."

– Truman Capote

THE OVERRIDING RULE, above anything else, is the Case Statement must be read. Nothing else counts.

Here are some tips that will be helpful. And a roster of some hoary no-no's I believe are not applicable to the Case Statement you will be writing.

There are times you may feel ambushed by Grammarians and Purists in great numbers, their shafts zinging from behind every tree in the forest. I know. I've been there.

(If anyone challenges you on any of my principles, just say: "It's okay. Panas says we can now do this. We have his permission." Just don't send me your nasty letters.)

The homily that follows I offer with prideful pleasure and

consummate confidence. Miss Breckenridge, my 11th Grade English teacher, would not approve.

1. It's perfectly all right to end your sentence with a preposition. There are some sentences that become unbelievably awkward if you try to avoid what Miss Breckenridge told you mustn't be done. (I take my cue from Winston Churchill who was asked about his use of the offending preposition. He wrote: "This is the sort of English up with which I will not put.")

2. It's acceptable to occasionally split infinitives. Some of our best writers do. By doing so, they find it possible to considerably improve the writing. And the reading.

3. I give you permission to start a sentence with And or But. And you can even start a paragraph with either of those two words.

   But not so often it becomes a standard of your writing.

4. You're allowed to have a one-sentence paragraph. There are times when just a one word paragraph is perfect to meet your needs.

   Really!

5. Contractions are allowed, at times even encouraged. But not when you are (instead of *you're*) trying to make a key point.

6. Review your copy to see if you can expunge the *thats*. In an earlier chapter, I first wrote: "Flaubert said *that* he wanted the writing to be so exciting *that* you could…" When I revised the sentence, I deleted the *thats*. Note how much stronger it is: "Flaubert said he wanted the writing to be so exciting you could…"

7. Don't use jargon and be very careful with initials and acronyms. You may understand them but you take the risk your readers won't.

8. An exciting Case Statement, whatever its length, seems short. The reader wants it to go on forever like a Beethoven chorale. A dull piece, no matter how few pages, is too long.

   Don't worry about what Churchill said: "This report, by its very length, defends itself against the risk of being read." A well written Case will be read. Whatever the length.

   By the way, Alexander Dumas' publishers paid him by the line. Can you imagine how full his dialogue would be if he were writing a Case Statement.

   "Pass the mustard."

   "Eh?"

   "I said, 'Pass the mustard.'"

   "You want some custard?"

   "No, mustard."

   "Oh!"

   Each carriage return would be a happy ring on the cash register.

9. Avoid the semi-colon; studies show it temporarily stops the reader and interferes with the flow and momentum.

10. Use the present tense as much as possible. There is vitality and zest in the present. Go back to my chapter on Bonnie McElveen Hunter. *I'm sitting* with Bonnie is more vital than *I was sitting,* or worse still: *I had been with* Bonnie.

11. Expunge the word, *Excellence*. It is so stagnated by overuse, it should be confined to naming goldfish.

12. Make your verbs sweat. They push the sentence forward and give it momentum. They add vitality and zest.

    Eschew adverbs. (Oh, all right. A few every 100,000 words.) Let the verb do the work for you. Follow Virginia Woolf's dictum to use words that soak up life.

13. Is it *who?* Or *whom?* Fess up. Do you have trouble with this. I do. I confess this to you only because I know you would understand.

    Take this sentence for instance: "There are hundreds of men and women *who* we must embrace in our program." Or is it: "There are hundreds of men and women *whom* we must embrace in our program."

    Fowler, the grammarian potentate, has four pages, single-spaced, devoted to this question. Read it. Read it again. You will still be confused. On the one hand, if it is the predicate of the subject followed by a transitive verb, it's *who*. On the other hand...oh, never mind.

    Here's what I find. Try it yourself and see how it works for you. Simply leave out the word *who* or *whom*. In most cases you can. It actually makes the sentence stronger. "There are hundreds of men and women we must embrace in our program." And it takes the curse off trying to determine *who* or *whom*. (You can send your letters of heartfelt appreciation for this suggestion to me in care of the Publisher.)

14. Be discriminate with the use of exclamation marks! The more you use them, the less BANG you get! Don't forget it! And if you feel you must use an exclamation mark, never use two!!

15. I try to avoid, "etc." That's a matter of personal preference and style. But even Fowler *(Modern English Usage)* agrees: "…to resort to using etc. is amateurish, slovenly, and incongruous." Well, that's a bit strong, but you get the point.

16. If it "goes without saying," then don't say it.

17. Never use, "As you know." Or, "As mentioned before."

18. It's not important what you put in. It is important what you leave out. "The test of good writing," Hemingway once said, "is how much good stuff you can leave out."

19. Instead of using bullets (•), number your items. Studies show that a listing with numbers stands-out and is read. (Although I've really challenged you with this long a roster.) Bullets are dull and listless— much as Miss Breckenridge's afternoon class on a warm spring day.

20. If possible, avoid a laundry list of projects and costs. That's what Nobel Laureate Patrick White called, "too many alternatives, and no choices." If you have a long list of numbers or facts, consider putting them in the Appendix.

21. After you have finished your First Draft, read the material out loud. If it sounds like writing, rewrite it. Don't let pretty words (what Elmore Leonard calls *hoopdedoodle*) get in the way of what you want to say.

22. This is not particularly relevant but somehow I can't resist mentioning it. George Will says, "never use a triple negative and that's not unmeaningless."

Write as if you are addressing your favorite aunt and the mechanic in the garage who works on her car.

Be scrupulous. Check for typos, misspellings, omitting important words, and columns of figures that don't add up. (Some accountant or engineer is certain to do the addition.)

If you get caught on even the most modest of infractions, the reader will challenge the entire document. (It will usually be your wealthiest potential donor whose name is misspelled.)

Proof your material. Proof it again. Imagine what havoc it must have caused among the bishops and priests (and gleeful abandonment among the parishioners) to come across the Seventh Commandment in the new edition of the Bible especially prepared for King Charles I. It read: *Thou shall commit adultery.*

Your type should be in *serif,* such as Times Roman. That's the font with all of the squigglies on the feet of the letters. Research indicates this font is the easiest read and remembered.

"Now, which of these fonts would Jerry choose?"

Here's more information researchers have found. Italics are more difficult to read than a regular font. Reverse italics, impossible.

Reverse printing is very attractive to use in a select and limited way. It looks pretty, but is demandingly difficult to read.

There is more that studies tell us. A sentence or a paragraph, or even a title, of all capital letters is formidable to read. If you want to use all caps (a style I like for titles and headings), make the initial cap of each letter a smidgen (this is the closest I can come to a technical term) taller.

I prefer paragraphs with no more than three sentences, four at the most. You probably gathered that in reading my first few chapters. You'll keep your reader's attention that way.

Consider run-on and complex sentences as treason to your writing. And to the reader.

Labor over your sentences. Polish their finish to lapidary sparkle.

Use short sentences. They are memorable. Six to nine words are great. Up to twelve, okay. Over thirteen and you're stretching the reader. Feel you are being paid by the period.

Take a lesson from *USA Today*. Look at their stories. The paragraphs are all one sentence. Their studies show those are the easiest to read and digest.

Write as clearly and unadorned as possible. "Use words everyone can understand," says Hemingway. In poetry and fiction, there may be a place for ambiguity, but never in a Case Statement. Follow Robert Frost's advice to John F. Kennedy, "to be more Irish than Harvard."

No one makes the point more effectively than George Orwell. He translates into gobblygook-fuzz this favorite verse from *Ecclesiates:*

"I saw that the race is not to the swift, or the battle to the strong, nor bread to the wise, nor riches to the intelligent, nor favor to the men of skill; but time and chance happen to them all."

Orwell's version goes:

"Objective consideration of contemporary phenomena compels the conclusion that success or failure in competitive activities exhibits no tendency to be commensurate with innate capacity, but that a considerable element of the unpredictable must invariably be taken into account."

I try to use words with no more than three syllables. If the reader cracks a tooth on a hard word in the Case, it's tough to swallow the writing that follows.

Take a lesson from Lincoln's powerful Second Inaugural Address. No one with a pulse can read it without boundless passion and awe. "Fondly do we hope fervently do we pray, that this mighty scourge of war may pass away…with malice toward none, and charity for all." And the most eloquent of all, only four single-syllable words long: "And the war came."

It was a marvel of economy with only 701 words. There were 505 words of one syllable and 122 of two syllables.

My strong preference is to enclose the Case Statement in a three-ring binder. Your material will be kept. (No one ever throws away a three-ring binder!) Put the name of your institution on the spine and the title of your Case on the front cover.

I recommend the three-ring binder to all my clients. We use it particularly for our very top donors. Yes, for our very largest donors. It gives the appearance of a low budget production. Yet it is functional and can be surprisingly attractive.

Make effective and frequent use of headings and subheadings. They add zest and give the reader a necessary breather. Too much copy without a break can cause reader-indigestion. Readers graze the material before they sit down for a full meal of reading.

Take a cue from the Wall Street Journal. Their four-tier headline helps introduce the whole story and their sub-heads are tantalizing. Here's an actual sample.

Some one at The New York Times must have thought it was a good idea, also. Note how effectively the multi-tiered headlines tell the whole story— all in just twenty-eight words. Bing, bing.

I use photographs throughout. One to each page is not too many. They must be compelling and tell a story. They should supplement, not detract from the text.

Proper cropping of the photographs is essential. This is best left to a bright and creative designer.

All photographs should have captions. (*Caption and captivating* have the same root.) Can you imagine a photograph in any magazine that doesn't have an interpretive and identifying caption.

The nicest thing a reader can say about your Case is: "You make me feel I am right there with you." That's what you're after. You want to push your writing to where vision meets commitment.

THE WALL STR

© 2003 Dow Jones & Cor

DOWJONES

Leap of Faith

Child's Rare Illness Leaves Her Parents With a Dilemma

Couple Did Lots of Research On Treatment—and Found Conflicting Opinions

Picking a Transplant for Molly

By AMY DOCKSER MARCUS

ARLINGTON HEIGHTS, Ill.—In December 2000, Jenny and John Birmingham learned that their 8-month-old daughter, Molly, had a rare genetic disorder called Hurler Syndrome. She would be dead by the age of 10, maybe sooner, the doctors said.

There were two treatments, both dangerous. Either one might just as easily kill her as save her. And even if one of the treatments worked, the Birminghams had no assurance that their daughter would live anything approaching a normal life.

The Birminghams had only a few months to make the choice. Data on Hurler's how children fare better if they

Busin

THE W
ask C
measures
nesses ad
pension f
sions a s
lieve som
ments bu
long term
term cha
nies with
and retir

■ Canada
hostile S
rival Pe
ate the v
company

■ Stocks
about th
jumped
dr

Printed in Chicago   ONE DOLLAR

NORTH KOREA SAYS IT HAS MATERIAL FOR ATOM BOMBS

INFORMS U.S. OF ITS PLANS

Bush Team Uncertain Whether Threat to Make Half-Dozen Weapons Is Just a Bluff

By DAVID E. SANGER

WASHINGTON, July 14 — North Korean officials told the Bush administration last week that they had finished producing enough plutonium to create a half-dozen nuclear bombs, and that they intended to move ahead quickly to turn the material into weapons, senior Ameri officials said today.

The new declara
scrambli

8

USE THE
"F" WORD

"On a good day, I stare at the wall for eighteen hours or so, feeling entirely terrible. And if I am lucky, a few words like NEVER or END or NOTHING will find a place on my blank sheet of paper."

– Samuel Beckett

I'M OFTEN ASKED ABOUT THE LENGTH of a Case Statement. Recently, I read in a professional journal that Case Statements should be no more than two or three pages long. The author says our busy prospects won't take time to read.

That's like saying the mark of a good Case Statement is to have a brilliant beginning, a brilliant ending— and keep them as close as possible.

Nonsense!

Question: How long should a Case Statement be?

Answer: As long as it needs to be. Not one page longer, not one page shorter.

Typically, in our firm, our writer's Case Statements run about twelve to fifteen typed pages. That's designed and with photos.

41

Here's what I find: If a Statement is several pages long and not well written, it won't be read. If it's fifteen pages and well written, it will be read.

Some board members will tell you donors won't read a Case if it's too long. It's only too long if it's not well written.

Even the ultimate musician Mozart had a problem in this regard. On the opening performance of *The Magic Flute,* a famous critic reported: "The opera is filled with too many notes."

I'm one with Robert Frost. My idea of Hell is a half-read Case Statement.

The answer therefore is to make certain it is well written. That is, of course, the key. "Speak on, but be not over-tedious," says Burgundy in Shakespeare's Henry VI.

But tell me how can you possibly engage the reader, describe the need, create the urgency, make the case, and motivate the prospect to give— all in just several pages.

I'm also asked who should prepare the Case Statement. I admit to a bias.

It can certainly be done by a member of the institution's staff. Often it is. Many organizations have writers who are extremely effective and powerful in their talent and ability. So writing it internally may be a good choice.

The problem in having a member of the staff prepare the Case is it almost always takes longer. Well, that's the truth of it.

If you really want to have somebody on the staff prepare the

Case Statement, make certain that he or she is relieved of any other responsibility and can spend full-time in the writing. Most staff writers will take three or four weeks. That's if they work full time on it.

In our own case, from the time we visit the site, prepare the material, provide the first draft, do our revisions, and get final approval— all of this requires about ten working days. Our writers prepare about a hundred of these a year, so we have a certain talent and experience for getting them done. Yet, each Case is inherently different.

Here's something that fascinates me. The quality of the writing is often dependent on the affection (yes, affection) the writer feels for the institution. It has to be a love affair. The writer has to be *simpatico* with everything, virtually "smothered" in its mission and service.

There are times when one of our writers returns from an assignment with sort of a ho-hum attitude.

"How did it go?" I ask.

"Oh, okay. They're doing a fine job, I guess."

On it goes like this. There's no passion. If the writer feels the organization is doing a so-so job, I know I'm going to get a so-so Case. Pablum.

Like the wild geese, I go elsewhere. I assign a new writer and start all over.

There are a number of issues in using the internal staff. I don't want to sound like a curmudgeon…

Wait, strike that. I do.

You may not have a staff person with as much experience as a professional writer. (And don't even think of using your grant writer. Writing a grant requires a different kind of writing.) Finally, using your own staff may make it more difficult to be objective and critical of the writing.

The other great advantage of using a professional is you get an outside perspective. This can be immensely revealing and exciting.

I think of what Howard Carter said when his lantern first beamed light into the cave that held King Tut's crypt. One of his group shouted: "Can you see anything?" "Yes, wondrous things."

You may find after you calculate the cost of your staff and their time, using an outsider is actually less expensive. What is terribly expensive is a poorly written Case.

But I protest too much. I've made it clear there are pitfalls in undertaking this internally or writing the Case yourself. Now that you've been warned— go for it. Try. Samuel Johnson was probably thinking of you when he said that once the itch of writing comes over a person, nothing will cure it but the scratching of a pen.

(If you do decide to write the Case— I want you to try— or write it internally, use this book as your religious guide. Just like Thoreau, "I perceive that I am dealt with by a superior power." Follow my book as you would the gospel! Underline, highlight, and write in the margins.)

I strongly suggest the CEO should not undertake the writing. Their input is essential for the review. And the editing, of course.

The flavor and special touches, yes. But not the writing. (There's one thing more. It's difficult to be critical of the CEO's writing: "Boss, I think your writing sucks.")

If you are the CEO and are a single-person staff, and have no funds at all for a professional, seek a volunteer who is a good writer. Failing that, forget everything I've said. Skip this particular section, and go back to chapter one and start reading all over again.

I like having anecdotes that demonstrate dramatically the impact of the organization. The wonderful Pueblo poet Simon Ortiz wrote: "There are no absolute truths, only stories." Use names, tell the story of how your organization has changed a life, or saved the life of one of your clients.

Quotations from key people are engrossing and engaging. In a very few sentences, quotations effectively drive home a point. They add zest. They make it come alive. The CEO, the chairman of the board, a client— you get the idea.

Think of whose imprimatur will provide high endorsement to the program. We've had a Catholic college where we used a quotation from a Cardinal. We have used the governor of a state. For one medical center, we used the President of the American Hospital Association.

The first draft of the Case Statement has to be shown to some of the leaders of the institution in order to get approval. I cover that in more detail later.

One very effective use, I find, is to give the approved Last Draft to the very top prospects— before it is in final printed form. It is an extraordinary cultivation tool. You ask for their counsel and advice regarding the piece. (I've mentioned this twice before. I repeat it because three times' the charm.)

Find the quotes, the scenes, the facts, the anecdotes that make for vital action. Write so they all intertwine to reveal the energy and excitement of the institution. You transform mission into results, dreams into reality.

The Case should demonstrate fervor if it is to be compelling. (Fervor. There, I've used the "F" word.) You write psalms of fervor and passion. Your job is to keep cranking the fly wheel that turns the gears that spin the belt in the engine of fervor.

The reader must share in the passion with you. "He must become susceptible and responsive to being thrilled," declares Mary McCarthy.

You become bound in commitment and devotion to the cause. The Case becomes a kaleidoscope of human action and energy that takes a thousand forms and works in a million wondrous ways.

You will be pleased I did not consider recommending the remarkable feat of Georges Pereck. The experimental French writer composed a 311-page novel without once using the letter *E*.

9

RUNNING
WILD

"These holy pages are produced in horrible pain. You do not know what it is to stay a whole day with your head in your hands trying to squeeze your unfortunate brain to find a word."

– Marcel Proust

THE CHINESE ARE PARTICULARLY WELL KNOWN for their gossamer-like design work. There is a formula in their theory of Classical Art which states: "White space counts more than black."

The principle is that a talented painter can enrich the imagination of an observer by means of the blank space he deliberately leaves on a painting. This makes what is not painted even more brilliant and vivid than what is.

That is precisely what you want to achieve. You allow the readers of your Case Statement an opportunity for their imagination to run wild.

It's no easy task, the writing. You want your reader to know by making a gift, they have the power to change things. It's their money, it's their decision. They want to see the impact of their gift. It's your job to make that happen.

Writing is difficult for me. That's because I'm not a professional writer. I don't wake up in the morning and think in the imperative about writing.

When I have the infrequent assignment, I know I've got to begin the writing, I've got to work on the writing, and I've got to finish the writing. I understand what a challenge it can be.

I can identify with Eudora Welty. She says, "I begin with the first sentence and trust to Almighty God for the second." Amen.

Picture a mountain with a sheer rock face like a pane of glass. So high it touches the sky. I find writing a little bit like climbing that mountain. I find only a desperate few handles in the mountain to hang on to.

Writing for me is like the climbing. You must begin.

You find leverage for fingers and toes. You start focusing a great deal of strength through small muscles you didn't know you had. You hold on and you push up and lean out. It's almost as if you are lying on the surface of the sea, trusting it not to take you under.

You don't look back. You don't look down. You keep on going.

You use your experience and intuition all at once. You do what you know well and you discover to your great surprise you find new resources you never knew you had.

"How do you write? You write, man, you write, that's how," says William Saroyan. And so, I begin. If I can do it, so can you. I'll tell you how I start my Case Statement.

Make believe you're writing to a friend. What would you say?

Dear Mary: I only today realized how desperate the need is in our community for a center for the homeless. I was walking home the other night and it was bitterly cold. You know how desperate it can get in Minneapolis in February. There were dozens— yes dozens— of homeless curled up in cardboard boxes. I simply couldn't believe it. I was all bundled up in a muffler and heavy coat and I was still shivering with cold. I don't know how these folks can survive. And it wasn't only men. Mary, I saw women and children. It broke my heart . . .

You get the point. Your Case Statement will have to be more formal than that, of course. But you do want to convey some sense of intimacy. (Remember, when writing a Case, you're writing for an audience of one.)

You do want to deliver zest and punch. You want to find a beautiful tune in your head and somehow translate that into words.

You think and write on the brink of exaltation. Some may think this obsessive, but obsession is another word for passion— passion with a fierceness.

There is truly very little writing genius. Few have that gift.

Good writing is simply the infinite capacity for taking pains. You write, you review, you revise. I call it the 3Rs. (Yea, okay. So I stretched a little!)

You learn to recognize what isn't important. Then, ignore and delete it. You act much like the sculptor who turns a block of marble into an elephant by chiseling away everything that doesn't look like an elephant. You chip away.

Complicated writing comes easily. Simplified writing actually takes a lot more work. Ernest Hemingway says he wrote the last page of *Farewell to Arms* thirty-nine times before he was satisfied.

Unlike Hemingway, you're probably not working for a Pulitzer. But your job is indeed to be endlessly inspirational. You motivate your donor to action.

The good news, if you find writing difficult, is that effective writing doesn't come easy for most— even the experienced. It requires a remarkable dedication to work, to slogging away at a problem and task.

It is almost never a matter of having a flash of divine inspiration. The dictionary is the only place where *success* comes before *work.*

We all write with a different style and momentum. Kurt Vonnegut says writers should be ruthless, relentless, and downright brutal with their prose, stripping it of everything that doesn't matter.

I have a confession. It's a problem, and I know it.

It's a horrible failing. When I review and revise, I don't take anything out. I keep adding and adding. One day I must learn: When putting cheese in a mouse trap, be certain to leave room for the mouse.

I'm not alone. John Irving says that, "finishing is more difficult than beginning. It takes more time to rewrite than it does to do the first draft. You have to be much more careful."

What I find is that somehow if you have proper focus and direction, it never comes to a bad end. The writing will ultimately come out where it should.

My problem is that I'm a reformed perfectionist— and I keep falling off the wagon. I can't help myself. I think of Beckett. He attached a card to the wall beside his writing table. On it were written the words: "Fail. Fail again. Fail better." I keep failing, revising, and rewriting. And sadly— adding.

All of a sudden I find an irrational exuberance. As E.M. Forster put it: "I am convincing in a surprising way."

I turn the corner in my mind, do a somersault, jiggle a creative kaleidoscope, and I don't know what else (let's have a drum roll). Then suddenly it all comes together. You achieve congruence with your reader.

If I can do it, you can too.

"Who the devil wrote this terrible Case Statement.
It comes dangerously close to the truth!"

10

GETTING READY

"Getting ready to write is the most painful experience you can imagine. I go from exasperation to a state of total collapse."

– Gustave Flaubert

IT WON'T BE LONG NOW. You'll be starting your writing soon. Here's how you begin.

You need to prepare, to discuss, and have on hand the items I list on the next few pages. At first blush, you'll feel you don't need all of these items. Take my word for it: You will.

This book is meant as a guide for you to work with and use. That's why I suggest you actually check the boxes. Go ahead, pick up a pen and check them off. Feel free, too, to write in the margins, underline, and make notes. I want this book to be a working tool for you.

Check-off the item when you have it actually in hand

❏ A brief history of your organization.

❏ The Mission Statement.

❏ Your organization's short-and long-range objectives and goals.

❏ Marketing or program plans developed to reach objectives and goals.

❏ The results of a recent market research study, if available.

❏ The annual budget of you organization including a breakdown of sources of support: i.e., corporate contributions, individual contributions, foundation grants, United Way revenue (if you are a member agency), and fees.

❏ A description of your major programs and a rationale of how these meet specific client needs.

❏ Membership or client information including statistics for individual program participation and the total number served. Information on membership or client demographics. It is helpful to have information about age, race, and income.

❏ Information on the giving sources within the community or your constituencies. Include those who have given in the past and sources you will target for the campaign or on-going fundraising. Any relevant research is particularly helpful here.

❏ Information on growing constituency or community needs your organization will address within the next few years. Statistics to support these claims help define these areas of need. The statistics will likely be transformed into graphs in the Case.

❏ Within the context of your organization's mission, how will the organization strive to meet these emerging needs? It is most effective to cite specific programs or initiatives and specific participation goals.

❏ Specifics on the fundraising program, including the total goal and the cost of any individual projects.

❏ Information on the role of the campaign and how the funds will translate into the people served, and lives changed and saved.

❏ Endorsements from recognized community leaders and appropriate government officials give life to the material and help build a persuasive case.

❏ Any characteristic of your programming, history, or individual relationships that the organization holds in esteem elevates the campaign's importance.

❏ The biography of the founders, the CEO, and your leaders who are key to the organization's vitality and success provide another human element.

❏ You will need to do some interviewing. These visits will probably take an hour each.

The interviews should include the Chair of the Board, one or two board members, any other appropriate staff, and one to three interviews with clients participating in programs you have identified as key to the campaign.

Interviews that illustrate how a client's life was enhanced or changed through your programs are particularly effective. This is also true for any interview demonstrating a special relationship between a supporter and staff member or volunteer.

Make a list of those you plan to interview.

❏ Photographs of the facility, staff, and clients working together, clients being served, and shots of those individuals to be interviewed. These help generate empathy for your cause.

In the Appendix, there is a much more complete list I want you to review. It will take only a few minutes to examine. It's what Rainer Marie Rilke called, "living the questions."

One thing more: Organize all your material before you start writing. If you don't, you'll be constantly shuffling and sifting piles of paper. "I must carefully prepare," says Norman Mailer. "If I don't, I spend my time thinking about what I should have for dinner. Then I make myself another drink."

Proper preparation and gathering this material in advance will save you hours in the writing. And you will have a more successful and effective Case Statement. My 5-Ps: **P**roper **P**reparation **P**rovides a **P**erfect **P**roduct.

Believe me, I've tried every shortcut. When I do, I usually find myself landing at JAIL (lose two turns) and then, "Return, go back to START.

I think of a couple lines from *Waiting for Godot*. They keep running through my mind. Estragon says: " I can't go on like this." Vladimir replies: "That's what you think."

Do I still have your attention. That is pretty boring stuff, all this preparation. Borrring!

Hemingway said: "The story I'm writing exists. I know that. It's written in absolutely perfect fashion. It is someplace, somewhere, in the air somewhere. All I must do is prepare. I prepare with painstaking care. Then I will find my story and then simply copy it."

Good. You're ready to begin. The day has finally come when the risk to remain tightly wound as a bud is more painful than the risk it takes to blossom.

11

YOU SIMPLY BEGIN

"Writing is a horrible, exhausting struggle, like a long bout of some painful illness. One would never undertake such a thing if one were not driven by some demon whom one can neither resist nor understand."

– Charles Dickens

WE HAVE AN OLD FARM HOUSE in West Cornwall, Connecticut. There's a Volunteer Fire Department.

I'm talking to the Chief one day. I ask him what his crew does first when they get to a fire. "Well, we immediately drench the house with water. Then we break open the windows to get our equipment inside. Break down a door if necessary."

"What do you do next?" I ask.

"We then check to make absolutely certain we have the right address."

You've done better. Everything is in order. You know while putting things off, life speeds by. You must begin.

It's easy to put things off. I can testify to that. Procrastination, like all long words, is the thief of time.

I've tried all the excuses. Here's a list of the ten effective ways I've found to put-off starting a Case Statement.

MY LIST OF THE TEN MOST EFFECTIVE WAYS TO PUT OFF WRITING THE CASE

1. Call a friend.

2. Check your e-mail and send some e-mails to relatives you haven't heard from for awhile.

3. Surf the Internet— check the news, weather, and the value of your stock.

4. Rearrange the piles on your desk.

5. Make a To-Do list.

6. Recite selected poems of Emily Dickinson.

7. Sharpen your pencils. (Hemingway sharpened 20 #2 pencils every morning before starting his writing.)

8. Pay bills and balance your checkbook.

9. Do the filing you've been putting off for several months.

10. Floss your teeth (this, by the way, is the most drastic of all— and should be considered only as a last resort).

E.B. White knows a thing or two about putting off the start of his writing. "I rise in the morning torn between the desire to improve the world...and the desire to enjoy the world. This makes it hard to plan the day."

It's amazing how much writing and work you can get done, if you really decide you're going to get started. There's an old Irish proverb that says: You'll never plough a field by turning it over in your mind.

I've invented a new Murphy's Law for putting off your writing: "Before you do anything, you find you have to do something else first."

Expect something special from what comes next. It's one of the great truisms of writing. Get ready to underline. It comes from Joseph Barbato, a professional Case Statement writer and one of the best. He says you never find the time to write. You have to make the time.

"You simply begin," says Susan Sontag. "You write by sitting down and writing. The trick is to make time, not try to steal it here and there."

The word "begin" is full of energy. You simply begin. You'll never finish if you forever keep beginning. Lewis Carroll had it right: "Alice thought to herself, 'I don't see how he can ever finish if he doesn't begin.'"

I follow the same advice I've heard about eating an elephant. You take one bite at a time. Nothing is particularly difficult if you divide it into small jobs.

It's easy for me because I'm an optimist. I begin. When I start writing I'm never really certain where I'm going or where I'll end up. But I'm on my way.

Let's begin.

Each writer has a style uniquely his own. (Okay, okay— you prefer..."a style uniquely his or her own.") I'd like to suggest a few things that are helpful to me. Keep them in mind. They will help you create a document with a sense of force and urgency.

Sell Your Reader. Don't lean over backwards to present your facts too objectively. Sure, tell the truth. Of course. But you must state your case in a manner that propels the reader to get out the checkbook.

You must motivate. You must ask for the order. You are the cheerleader.

Make your organization look as if it has been destined since the beginning of time to address this very special challenge and at this very moment in history.

Appeal First to the Emotions— then to the Intellect. Personalize statistics with true stories and case studies. Resist the mundane.

Write about a specific heart patient or a girl who was able to continue her education only because of the scholarship she received at the college. Tell about Mary, a child born with cerebral palsy who takes her first step. Use the dramatic story about Johnny, a delinquent, whose life was turned around by the Boys Club.

Don't be subtle. Be specific, use names. If it makes the reader tingle and break out in goose bumps…well, you're on your way to a gift!

Hone Your Words Painstakingly. Some words are more positive, more powerful than others. Make your words inch-perfect. When you are talking about the project, say what wonderful things it *makes* possible (Not *would make* or *will make* possible).

Never ask for help. Instead, talk in terms of the exciting opportunity the program presents to the donor. Write about the important investment a donor can make and how huge the dividends are.

Be brief about expressing the problems. Devote more time to your solutions. Donors want to hear the good news, positive outcomes, and results that count.

Focus on the incredible work being accomplished in a less than adequate facility. That's better than describing a place so squalid and unsafe the organization couldn't possibly be doing a decent job.

Punctuate your Case with opportunities. Be a possibility thinker and writer.

Don't worry a heck of a lot about the difference between a goal and an objective. I've never found anyone who cares. Just make certain the reader understands what problems you plan to solve. And how.

Don't use the word, pledge. Do you remember how much fun it was to get a gift at Christmas or on a birthday? A gift is fun, with very positive connotations. A pledge, a contribution, even a donation, do not have the same warm-fuzzies as the magic word: Gift.

Using precisely the right word is strikingly important.

Question: What's the difference between ignorance and indifference.

Answer: I don't know and I don't care.

Break the Copy with Interesting Headings and Sub-Heads. Give readers a chance to pause and catch their breath.

Tell Your Readers What You Want Them To Do. If your Case is being used for a feasibility study, say that the institution welcomes the interviewee's ideas and involvement.

If the case is used as the principal campaign publication, win their hearts. Then ask specifically for their participation.

Be Certain to Use Visual Aids and Quotations. Maps, graphs, photographs, and charts add high impact to the Case. "What is the use of a book," thought Alice, "without pictures and conversations."

Use quotations from the institution's "users," and well-known citizens in the community who endorse the project and the institution. There are many who can speak to the need for the project.

Or search for a famous author, an artist, philosopher, or an expert in the institution's field of service. This will underline the importance of your message and add credibility. It's what is called, "working near the heart of things."

Remember, the Case Statement should move the reader to action. Tell them what you want them to do.

If it is sufficiently dramatic and appealing, the Case transforms the institution into a cause, and the cause into a crusade. And crusades are what motivate men and women to action.

You've started the writing and you'll keep on going. If Columbus had turned back, no one would have blamed him. But no one would have remembered him, either.

When you first began, you thought it would be just about as easy as staging a full ballet in a telephone booth. But you've now lanced the boil. You understand St. Thomas when he said: "A beginning truly seems to be more than half of the whole because all of the rest is contained virtually in it."

You may not be as driven as Isaac Asimov, but now you can sympathize. He said: "Thinking is the activity I love best, and writing is simply thinking through my fingers. I can write up to eighteen hours a day. I've done better than fifty pages a day. Nothing interferes with my concentration. You could put on an orgy and I wouldn't even look up— well maybe once."

"Wow! What a glorious day to begin writing a Case Statement."

12

THE THREAD
THAT BINDS

Mary Gordon, the gifted writer, says she can't imagine a writer con-
templating a day's work without dread. "Every morning, I wake up
and know that I've got to shoot that bear between the eyes."

IN A MOMENT, I'm going to tell you about the most exciting and attention-getting title I ever penned. But first let me tell you the purpose of the Case Statement's title.

The title casts the theme and spirit of the Statement. It is the melody you sing throughout. You want it to be sufficiently bold it captures the imagination and piques the fascination of the reader. It should enfold them in a dance of intrigue in which neither you nor the reader can escape the others' embrace.

You want it to be the kind of theme you can use throughout the piece. Its force swells with impact each successive time it's used. Like crashing cymbals.

The title is the thread that connects everything to everything. It ties the entire Case Statement together, from beginning to end. If there's a disconnect, you lose the reader.

I think of the title as a loose thread you keep pulling from your sweater. You have the sinking feeling you'll never be able to fix or finish what you're undoing. All the while, you're keenly aware you cannot, for the life of you, stop unraveling it.

The title has to have zest, exuberance, and a certain element of surprise. It has to be as beguiling as a firefly on a June night.

Avoid the trite and wishy-washy humdrum (apathy is rampant, but who cares!). What you seek is a WOW response. It should burn itself into the minds and hearts of your readers.

Your computer will automatically crash if the term, *Commitment to Excellence* is used for the title or written more than twelve times on a single page.

The paramount role of the title is to get the reader into the first few paragraphs of the Case. It has to be powerful enough and sufficiently stirring to get them to turn to page one. If it isn't, the chances are good you have lost them.

You want them to turn the page. You want to say to the reader, let me take you by the hand. Join me. There is something very special going on here. I want you to see it for yourself. I want to show you. Come with me.

Every writer has a different method. I like coming up with a title quite early so I can use it as a theme throughout. There are many times I come up with the title first of all, before I even start the writing. I make the copy fit it if the title is powerful enough.

There are other times my mind is a totally blank chalkboard. Nothing comes up on the slate. I find I don't get ideas, ideas get me.

It happens. There are times, no matter how I agonize, a brilliant idea for a title escapes. If that's the situation, I finish the Case and read it carefully. And reread it again if necessary. I look frantically for a handle, for something I can grab.

Somehow, there's always a word or a phrase that pops out. It never fails. Like Sherlock Holme's *Purloined Letter,* it was always there, right in front of my eyes, just waiting for me to spot it.

Then I test it for excitement, intrigue, and POW. If it holds up, I usually rewrite the first paragraph and the closing statement, weaving it into the copy. I manage to use it selectively throughout the document.

The concept for the title is a little like playing a pinball machine. It may need a bit of careful slamming and shaking to light up. Then all of a sudden, a *Coup de Foudre*— A strike of lightning.

I like a title that's one or two words— three or four at the most. No semi-colon, no sub-title. If the words are one or two syllables, all the better.

If it's really appropriate (*really* being the operative word), you should feel free to use something you've seen before. Just so your readers haven't. You may want to change or invert a word or two.

Oscar Wilde said you haven't really stolen it if you can't remember the source or who you stole it from. Just make certain that it fits perfectly for your situation.

One wag said to me that creativity is a virtue, but plagiarism is faster. She had just copped a magnificent title from another case.

In the Appendix, I list over a hundred titles I've used in the past few years.

Getting the perfect title is sometimes like getting dressed up for a party. You're unsure of what to wear right up until the last minute, frantically trying on one garment after another, not being able to make up your mind which combination looks really great.

Oh, yes. You perhaps have been wondering. I mentioned at the beginning of this chapter I had a title I consider the most striking I have ever used. It was for the Chicago Missionary Society. I called it: FOR CHRIST'S SAKE!

The theme and feeling I was trying to convey, of course, was that everything the Missionary Society did was for the Kingdom. I wasn't unmindful, either, of the double meaning. I found that the Baptists felt it wicked, and the wicked felt it wonderful.

Another title I used I'm particularly fond of is: CHRIST'S SMALL HANDFUL. This was written for a Methodist Seminary. I wanted men and women to know they could be among a very select group who could join Him by supporting the Seminary.

I'm not talking about razzle-dazzle, moving the shells faster and faster and faster, so that the prospect can barely keep track of the pea. But I do want to capture the attention and the heart of the reader.

When we did a Case Statement for a school with the title, SCHOLARSHIP ON FIRE— our prime donors kept talking about how powerful the title was. They were enthralled, captured.

The beguiling title leads right into the first and early paragraphs. This is where you wile your reader in a stranglehold he will never be able to break. He will be held captive throughout the document. These early paragraphs are where you make the reader your prisoner.

Nothing is more crucial than the early paragraphs. This is where you, the potentially all-powerful writer, must convince the potentially spellbound reader that this program is worthy of their attention, trust, and philanthropic desire.

You coax, entice. Continue to build. Every paragraph amplifies the one that precedes it. The last sentence is the springboard to the paragraph that follows.

Next to the opening paragraph, and the few that follow, the closing few paragraphs usually take me the longest to write. You want it to be the dream that glows and electrifies. Most of all, you want to move the reader to action. It's what the poet Martin Tupper wrote was, "a call from God to waken men."

When I write a particularly powerful close, I feel like I'm floating in space. You know the feeling. You've been there. You're completing a sequence of *fouettés* ending with a *triple pirouette*.

I always return to the theme in my closing. It solemnizes the marriage. It binds the invincible vision of the organization to the now-ready investor. The winds rise, the whitecaps swell. The reader hears the anthem of the call.

The theme seduces, the content accelerates the romance. The closing consummates the nuptials.

Using the theme to complete the Statement provides proper closure to the Case. It is the finish. It is the kind of accelerating, propelling wriggle a vacuum cleaner cord makes in retracting into its place of storage.

Seize the reader. Make the title an unforgettable embrace.

"I've got the revisions and suggestions to the first draft."

13

WRITE FOR A
SIXTH GRADER

"No one can understand how agonizing it can be. I'm not a 'born' writer. What I am is a good writer. I never get anything right the first time. I just know how to revise. But to begin my writing, there is that tortuous moment with that first page of paper that awaits the first sentence, even the first word. This clean piece of paper becomes your enemy. There is something excruciating about beginning. I mean every beginning. No matter how much you have written in the past, you begin all over as a student again. It can rip away at your ego."

– John Irving

I AM AT A BOARD MEETING of a very well known agency in Omaha. They're talking to me about a sizable campaign.

I probe and ask lots of questions in order to determine the state of their readiness. In the course of the discussion, the chairman says: "I thank God that we've never changed our Mission Statement, not one word, not in the eighty years of our existence."

You think I'm exaggerating. But in my astonishment at hearing the chairman, I write down everything as quickly as I can remember, word-for-word.

I'm thinking: I don't know very much about this organization but I judge this campaign is in trouble from the start. The world has changed inside-out in eighty years. Good grief, it's changed dramatically in the last twelve months.

This organization hasn't recognized the ever-ticking acceleration of change. If their Mission Statement is the same as it was eighty years ago, the parade has likely passed them by.

The Mission Statement provides the *why* that inspires every *how*. It provides the roadmap, the signposts for the organization's existence and its performance.

The board of an organization must be unabashed fools, head over heels, for the mission of the organization. It should burn in their bones like fire. It's the secret of the organization's success that the board have this passion for the mission. Unbridled, unflinching, and undying passion.

The single most significant reason people tell us they give is they believe in the mission of the organization. Nothing else comes even a close second.

These donors want to know: What does the organization say it does? And then: Does it actually do what it says it does? Does it practice what it preaches? They want to know if your actions are consistent with your words.

Here's my Rule for institutions. Know who you are, Say who you are, Do what you say you are. That's what donors want.

Circumstances do not make the organization and the mission does not make the organization. They reveal it. It defines your purpose and at the same time, shapes your destiny. Flaubert could have been referring to a Mission Statement when he said: "It's the main dish of existence."

You may wish to include the Mission in the Case Statement. But it's not necessary.

What? Not include the Mission Statement?

Well, okay. If you feel compelled to have it, include it in the section that deals with your organization's history. Actually, I like putting both the history and the mission near the end, but before the dramatic close of the Statement.

But here's what I want you to note. If the Mission Statement is dull or difficult to understand, or worse still is outdated— consider revising it or paraphrasing it, using snippets here and there.

Even that isn't necessary. You may wish only a few sentences to paraphrase your mission and indicate your purpose, using dramatic and powerful words.

Somewhere in the Case Statement you do need a description of your institutional objectives. These are the imperatives that propel you, and the service priorities that define you.

These describe the philosophy and focus of your operation which make you invincible. It's what George Bernard Shaw identified as, "the joy of being used for a purpose recognized by all as a mighty cause."

You need to indicate your uncommon objectives are unlike that of any other organization, and you provide a service different than any other institution. That is what will make you fundable. No one, not any other organization, does its work as effectively as you.

This is the platform which launches your program, and gives heart and character to the service you provide. I'm not talking about sloganism. I'm not suggesting the refrain from the show-stopper *Gypsy*: "You've got to have a gimmick."

Take a moment to read this Mission Statement of the *Los Angeles Times*. It is quite special, but most notable in one regard. I'll explain at the end.

> *We improve the performance of society by enriching, inspiring, invigorating, and educating our diverse communities. We are a trusted voice, providing compelling information through a living partnership with our readers, advertisers, employees, and shareholders. We excel by investing in our people in a dynamic work environment thriving on integrity, mutual trust, innovation, creativity, and teamwork.*

Did you notice something quite special? The Statement contains fifty-seven well chosen, carefully crafted words— not one of which is the word, *news*.

A Mission Statement is the life of your organization. It is what transforms your dogged determination into results. Here are nine points to consider.

1. The statement of your mission is an enabling and empowering document. It is the fuel that powers the engine that propels your institutional train.

    It uniquely combines your ethos, rationale, and philosophy. The Mission Statement memorializes, and at the same time places into action, your uncompromising purpose.

2. It describes your mission in a compelling way. I love the word, compelling. It comes from the Latin words: *com* (meaning: "together") and *pellere* (meaning: "to get or bring about by force or power").

   Purpose is when you make an unyielding commitment to do something. When you put these two words together (compelling and purpose), you provide the energy that sustains the spirit and promise for your organization.

3. Putting into precise words this institutional covenant can be fiercely awesome. It requires deep introspection, careful scrutiny, and clear expression.

   It becomes your conscience and your guide. It is the overriding criterion by which you monitor and measure the health of your organization. It provides direction, determination, and dedication to all programs and services you offer.

4. The Mission Statement needs to describe how your organization chooses to bring about change. It is not described in terms of the programs and objectives necessary to achieve change. It is the change itself that becomes your mission.

5. The clutter and clang of an overly long Mission Statement makes it impossible to find the kernel of the Statement itself. Keep it brief. Hone the words until there isn't any fat left.

6. The Statement should be understandable. If a sixth grade student can read, comprehend, and explain the Statement, you are probably on the right track.

7. The Statement should be reviewed, discussed, and approved by the Board of Directors. It should then be assessed on a

regular basis to make certain both your institution and the Mission continue to be relevant and in concert, one with the other.

8. Once the Mission is approved, it becomes the organization's credo, its anthem, the hymn it continually sings— with gusto, conviction, and zeal.

9. If you cannot breathe life and vitality into your Mission Statement, then decide to paraphrase it in your Case Statement. Use words that have faith and hope, conviction and audacity.

"From now on, our troubles will be out of sight," sings Judy Garland in *Meet Me in St. Louis.* If you follow these nine steps, the reader becomes an expert witness and roaring advocate for your organization.

14

STATISTICS AND DAMN LIES

"I am tired. I am exhausted. I am emptied dry. I spent the whole morning putting in a comma, and the whole afternoon taking it out."

– Oscar Wilde

"SINCE NOTHING IS PROVED, everything can be proved." Regard carefully those words of Albert Camus.

Let's be honest. Camus is one of literature's most quoted authors. But do you truly understand everything he writes? I'm embarrassed to admit (and I do so only because you and I are friends) that I don't. I don't, for instance, understand the quotation I just gave you. But I thought it seemed to be quite appropriate for this chapter on facts and statistics.

This is what I know. Research and data are the bricks which lay a path to your successful Case Statement. As Leslie Stephen said of Defore: "He provides a dazzling fascination in his clear recitation of the facts."

It is the integrity of sheer facts that provide the substantiation and build the pillars to support it. This, in spite of what Benjamin Disraeli said: "There are lies, damn lies— and statistics."

In my Case Statements, I'm very careful about the statistics I use. I much prefer inspiring and convincing anecdotes about a few of the clients, students, members who are served. Statistics have all the spontaneity and passion of barbed wire.

The typical reader doesn't have the time nor patience to slog his way through a sludge of statistics. Find the quotes and the anecdotes that provide action and feeling. This is what will more effectively reveal the institution.

> *It was late. I turned off the lights in my office and began walking home. I was crossing the quadrangle when I felt a hand on my arm. It was one of our students. It was obvious she wanted to talk. Let me tell you about Mary. It is one of the most extraordinary stories we have had at the College. When Mary first came to us as a student...*

You get the idea. Something like that is so much more striking than saying, "We have a third of our student body who are on some type of scholarship." As the British essayist Matthew Arnold said: "An example is not a little thing."

I call it the Anne Frank phenomenon. It's hard to imagine three million Jewish children killed in the Holocaust. The number is simply a statistical glob. But you can identify with Anne Frank. When writing, think *Anne Frank.*

Don't boil the ocean is another way of saying, you shouldn't try to analyze everything. But used appropriately, and sparingly, statistics can be effective in helping you make the case. It's what Hemingway called, "the one true thing."

Let's say, for instance your student body has increased dramatically each year for the last ten years, or your membership has skyrocketed fifteen percent each year for the last five years, or your admissions to the Emergency Room have grown exponentially in the last three years. All of these lend themselves effectively to statistics and a graph.

If the statistics are impressive, you should use them. It is what Walter Carpenter, former CEO of DuPont, referred to as, "the eloquence of facts."

A graph in a Case Statement has tremendous impact. In our readership studies, we find they garner far more attention than even the most dramatic photographs.

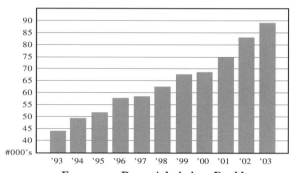

**Emergency Room Admissions Double
in the Last Ten Years**

I like to think you use your statistics as a drunk uses a lamppost— for support rather than complete illumination. They help you avoid the vulnerability of jumping a chasm in two leaps. (Eschew the incremental and go for the big leap.)

"There's something fascinating about statistics and graphs," said Mark Twain. "One gets such wholesome returns of conjecture out of such a trifling investment of fact."

Review all of the figures and statistics. If there is something that stands out and lends itself to a graphic display, go for it. Just avoid the eye-glazing listing of rows of statistics.

I'm reminded that Chicken Little acted before her research was complete. Statistics and data are important because they provide the platform for why the projected program is essential. They substantiate the results that can be expected. They place you at the intersection of who you are and who you want to be.

Coleridge calls it, "the willing suspension of disbelief." Statistics are your launching pad. They somehow ignite the organization's need with an emotional blaze. The canvas is neutral but the details and data are fluorescent.

Just make certain you use statistics with great discretion and inordinate care. They must never dominate, must never overshadow. The more you run over a dead cat, the flatter it gets. But used properly and sparingly, they help build the case. (Oscar Wilde warns the writer against, "falling into the careless habits of accuracy.")

There are three elements that are necessary for a persuasive and compelling case. Get out your highlighter again. These are essential.

1. **Relevancy.** The need for the proposed program and the funds you seek must be relevant. The case you build and substantiate must be faultless and impregnable.

   Without the proper data and substantiation, your case is just mutton dressed as lamb. There cannot be the smallest crack an unanswered question can squeeze into.

   In order to make certain you demonstrate relevancy, you need facts, details, and back-up information. This is where statistics lend a helping hand.

   You can't fake relevancy. That would be like what former Governor of Texas, Ann Richards, described as, "putting lipstick on a pig and calling her Monique."

2. **Allure.** The case for your program must have dramatic and emotional appeal. It has to sizzle.

   Almost any program for children can be made irresistible and compelling. That's a cinch. You'll be able to easily add *snap, crackle, and pop* to what you write.

   On the other hand, developing the case for buying a piece of property may require more imaginative writing on your part. Constructing a boiler room or taking care of a growing indebtedness, even more innovative packaging on your part.

   Be creative. A monk asks a superior if it is permissible to smoke while praying. The superior says, "absolutely not." The next day the monk asks the superior if it is acceptable to pray while smoking. "That is not only permissible," says the superior, "it is admirable." Packaging is everything.

   I am having lunch with Mary Kay in Dallas. She chaired a major campaign we managed. She says: "You know, Jerry, at Mary Kay, we don't sell cosmetics."

   "You don't?"

   "No...we sell hope."

   Now that's what I call creative packaging.

   Statistics won't really help you in adding dramatic appeal. They will, at times, open the door a crack for you. The great film director Fellini said: "Sometimes if you pull a little tail, you will find an elephant at the other end."

   Statistics, no matter how striking, will not trigger the spirit of the reader. Or the purse!

3. **Urgency.** There is nothing more important to your case than stressing and building an unrelenting sense of urgency. Nothing is more important (underlined, exclamation mark). Heidegger says urgency is at the source of everything.

   Consider this the Rosetta Stone of this book. You must create an unambiguous and resolute declaration of the solemn urgency of your program. The project cannot be put off. There is too much at stake.

   Yours is a program that must be undertaken and supported now. Now! Time will not wait.

   It's what philosopher-longshoreman, turned writer, Eric Hoffer, called, "things which are yet not." That's what selling the dream is all about.

   That's your job— to punch the gravity of the situation. You make the reader understand the circumstances are dire. *It is February and we are having sub-zero weather. If we don't have the funds now, there will be 450 children on our streets tonight without dinner or shelter.* That's the sort of thing I have in mind.

   This is one place statistics can be a welcome friend— when substantiating urgency. It provides assurance that there is integrity in your case. I say, even if your mother says she loves you— make her prove it.

You are the vision maker. Your writing will have freshness, energy, and reverberation of voice. You are the forceful and finite conduit of response. You are the artist. You continually take the reader's pulse. There is nowhere for the reader to hide.

15

A COMMITTEE
REVISES THE COPY

*"I get a warm feeling when I'm doing well. But that pleasure is
negated by the pain of getting started. Every morning, there's that
first sentence. The first word! Let's face it, writing is pure hell."*

– Stephen King

"WHEN I USE A WORD," Humpty Dumpty said, in a rather
scornful tone, "it means just what I chose it to mean—
neither more nor less." Lewis Carroll understood a thing or two
about revising.

Writing a Case Statement is a strange phenomenon. It involves
passion and endurance, a rare combination of desire and grunt
work. All this is often at odds with each other. Perhaps, in some
cases like a long marriage.

The Book of Common Prayer has it right. It has us offer thanks
for the means of grace and the hope of glory. You wonder what is
the more difficult. Is it tougher to write the Case Statement or
protect it against the committee who wants to revise it.

Something mystifying takes place when a group is asked to
review or edit a Case Statement. It kindles qualities in a person

somewhere between belligerence and sadism.

"No passion in the world," said H.G. Wells, "is equal to the passion to alter someone else's draft." There's something uncontrollably satisfying in reworking material. Someone else's material.

Let me offer a slight digression. I'll get back in a moment to the review and revision of your copy.

What follows is a revision of Lincoln's Gettysburg Address after a committee and board members (but certainly not your organization) were asked to look it over.

FOUR SCORE AND SEVEN YEARS AGO
should be eighty-seven years and four months ago

OUR FATHERS
confusing...do you mean the Pilgrims, or those who signed the Declaration of Independence, or what

BROUGHT FORTH On
"founded" would be a better

This Continent, A NEW NATION
be specific and name the country

CONCEIVED In Liberty And Dedicated To The
sounds awkward...better say "based on the idea of freedom"

Proposition That All MEN Are Created Equal.
tsch! tsch! what about women...we can't afford to upset the women

NOW WE ARE ENGAGED IN A GREAT CIVIL WAR Testing
make this the first paragraph— taking too long to get to the point

WHETHER THAT NATION OR ANY NATION
not necessary... just say "our nation"

So Dedicated And So CONCEIVED
there you go using "conceived" again...say "established"

Can LONG ENDURE.
endure what...a better term would be "continue to exist"

We ARE MET
mixed tenses, very bad...say "have met" or "are gathered"

On A GREAT BATTLEFIELD Of That War.
what battlefield...why not use the specific name

We Have Come To Dedicate A Portion Of That Field As A FINAL RESTING PLACE For Those
why beat around the bush...just say "cemetery"

Who Here Gave Their Lives THAT THAT Nation Might Live.
"that that" sounds like "ratatat-tat"...how about "that our country"

"Sorry, Mr. Lincoln, but you better try again. What we're after is something that's hard hitting with more punch. Something with more snap, crackle, and pop. More authoritative and forceful. Something impressive— something people will read and remember.

"By the way, would you mind using a little better scratch paper. It's hard reading your notes from those used envelopes."

Back to your Case.

It will happen. Count on it. You will have to submit your captivating manuscript to a committee for review. There is no great or small decision to which an organization will respond without a committee meeting.

Here is your verity for the day: If you want to kill the writing, get a committee working on it. They don't know what they want and won't be happy until they get it. You suffer the butterflies of the Gladiator squinting at the Emperor's box for a *thumbs-up* or *a thumbs-down.*

If you have an easily bruised ego, writing may not be the right career choice for you. This is no place for sissies. The key to a happy life for a Case Writer is to know how to deal with Plan B.

I've been there. In fact, many times. I can attest to the distress first-hand. "I know the pain. I have been here before," writes Rossetti.

I remember vividly one Case I presented to the committee of a major university. I thought the writing was consecrated, as irreproachable, for instance, as the stationery of a prestigious law firm or the presentation of a menu by a French head waiter.

I pass out copies for the committee to read. I watch the chair, as she turns the pages. Page one, page two. When she gets to page three, she has the expression of someone about to undergo root canal surgery.

"I don't like it!"

(I'm thinking of her as the Queen of Hearts in *Alice in Wonderland.* She is ready at any moment to shout, "Off with his head.")

Good grief. It's only page three, and she says she doesn't like it. The man next to her chimes in. He doesn't like it either. I start reciting the German Creed, *Gottes Strafe:* God's Punishment.

Few things are more upsetting than getting a second opinion you don't like any better than the first. I am stalled, like a badly fueled propeller blade. It's what John Steinbeck described as, "the urge to be somewhere else."

Then someone at the meeting says: "I don't want to be a devil's advocate but…" (Don't you hate hearing that? You know what's coming. A devil's advocate is the guy who rocks the boat, and then persuades everyone else there is a storm at sea.)

Well…grmph! I can see I'm not going to win this one. *Farmisched* is a Yiddish term for being completely knocked on your keister. Quick, Plan B.

I'm breaking out in a discernible tic.

I feel like the old woodsman who gives advice about catching a porcupine. "Watch for the slapping tail as you dash in and drop a large washtub over him. The washtub will give you something to sit on while you ponder your next move."

Do you feel the same as I do? You think of the Cheyenne-warrior battle cry: "It is a good day to die." You begin to feel there are evil spirits working on you at this very moment. What you considered as unalterable as the Holy Writ— is being profanely dismantled.

Even if you're right, you can't win. (Justice always prevails…three times out of seven!) It's what George Orwell once called, "the power of facing unpleasant facts."

Stop. I know the feeling but…you listen, you nod, you may even agree. What I've found is that if a committee doesn't feel excited and motivated by your precious copy, something may indeed be sorely wrong.

Keep in mind that the First Draft is the down-draft. You get everything down. The Second Draft is the up-draft. You fix it up. You follow the dictum of Camus: "That which does not kill you makes you stronger."

If it takes a Third Draft, chances are you're in serious trouble. Trying to patch it up at this point will be as successful as rebaking a fallen souffle. You may want to start all over.

I call this "Panas' Law of Diminishing Results": Once a Case Statement is fouled up and many times reworked and revised, anything done to improve it makes it worse.

I don't like submitting my material to a committee. Members of a committee that review someone's writing are, as described by John Steinbeck, people who go into the streets after a battle and shoot the wounded.

But let's face it— that's probably what will most likely happen. (Remember, I told you this isn't for sissies.) Someone once asked Clarence DeMar, seven-time winner of the Boston Marathon, to expound on his racing philosophy. "Run like hell, and get the agony over with."

You must have the strength and endurance to bear the wild ideas of others. (Guess what? At times, they are right.)

Frank Sinatra's song becomes your hymn: "Every time you find yourself flat on your face, pick yourself up and get back in the race." Move on, persist, and prevail.

There is a beautiful and joyous tune in your head. Now it's your job to translate that into words. You are the dream merchant.

16

BIGGER THAN
YOUR INSTITUTION

One of the earliest plays on record (492 B.C.) is called, 'The Capture of Miletus.' It was written by Phrynichus. The play was composed for production at Athens' great annual civic festival— a kind of Fourth of July, Veteran's Day, and Tony Awards all rolled into one. Given the extraordinary patriotic context, 'Capture' should have been a sure thing. But Phrynichus got more than he bargained for. According to the records, the Athenians were so distraught after seeing the play they fined the Playwright a huge sum. They forbade him future performances and told him that he would never be allowed to write again.

I'M GOING TO GUESS YOUR AGE. At least within a decade. I'll explain a little later.

You've read in a professional journal or perhaps a book— that the case for your project should be bigger than the institution itself. But I haven't found anywhere an explanation of what that means.

I'll tell you.

We're raising money for the Tampa Museum of Art. The

community will provide the funds to build a glorious new building downtown on the Hillsborough River.

The Museum will be able to exhibit its full collection in this new building. It will bring out of storage enrapturing pieces it does not now have the space to exhibit. It will finally have the space it needs.

It is estimated the Museum will attract an additional 200,000 people a year in the new facility. Many of this number will be young people.

The new building is obviously important to the future of the Museum.

But the case for the building is far more powerful and compelling than just a new facility for the Museum. For the first time, the Museum will be able to bring young people to see the full collection. They will grow in their understanding and appreciation of important art.

By the busloads they will come. By the thousands.

In your mind's eye, picture those grade school kids getting off the bus, lining up at the entrance. Eager. Curious. Starry-eyed. See them working the hands-on displays. The whoop and waggle. The excitement. It will be glorious.

So the case is for the young people of the area.

Well, there's more.

The Museum is on a gorgeous site on the River. Think of some of the positive environmental issues at play.

The new building will enhance the River Walk. There will be

elaborate landscaping and garden trails down to the river. A rather commonplace section of the Hillsborough River will be transformed into something endlessly inspirational.

But wait. The miracle isn't yet finished. There's still more.

The Museum will bring thousands of families back into a fatigued downtown. It will be the centerpiece of a new cultural and arts area. It will reinvigorate and transform downtown. Anyone with a modicum of care, pride, and responsibility for the Tampa area will have to support this project— whether they're interested in art or not.

And think of this. There is the infusion of money and people for the downtown merchants.

You see where I'm going with this. All of a sudden, the program becomes of much greater and multi-magnified consequence than just creating a facility to house more art.

You're not just a writer. You transform dreams into deeds. You search for every felicitous possibility that will make the project more expansive and worthy than the organization itself. Any crack that will open a new door.

You gather all of the information, you interview the key players, you begin developing your strategy for the writing. You may even be thinking of a possible title.

It's your job to put all of this into a package and develop an undeniable, irresistible, and urgent case for support.

Just keep in mind that a person doesn't go to a hardware store to buy a drill because they need a drill. They go to a hardware store to buy a drill— because they need a hole.

91

That's what you have to keep focused on. Is it the drill you'll be writing about or the hole? Your task is to make the case bigger and more encompassing than the organization itself.

And now, back to my promise I would guess your age. At least within a decade. Here's my question. Do you recognize the name: *The Presidential Yacht Potomac?*

If you do, you're around seventy-five. Probably a little older.

The Potomac was Franklin D. Roosevelt's yacht. He used it regularly during his presidency and especially the period of World War II. It was his release.

Some very significant meetings took place on the Yacht— with Churchill, Eisenhower, the Queen of England, the Prime Minister of Canada, and on a number of occasions his War Cabinet.

It would cruise up and down the Potomac for no more than a stretch of two or three miles. And then back again.

The Newsreels (are you old enough to remember those?) regularly featured FDR and a dignitary. Or just the President fishing, with that familiar floppy hat perched on top of his head.

During the stressful and weary days of the War, the dateline of news stories and radio broadcasts regularly carried the identification: *From the Presidential Yacht Potomac.*

You couldn't grow up in that era without feeling the Yacht was part of your life. That's why it is so easy to guess your age.

When Roosevelt died, the Potomac was put in dry-dock. Then not long after the War, a year or two, President Truman sold the Yacht. The name was lost.

Wait, that's not the end of the story.

The boat was discovered in a shipyard a dozen years ago and purchased by a nonprofit group. The boat had a number of owners since the days of FDR and was renamed several times. But in a special ceremony, it was re-christened by the nonprofit— *The Presidential Yacht Potomac.*

The boat was in terrible shape. It had to be completely renovated and made sea-worthy.

We were asked to raise the funds for the restoration. Jimmy Roosevelt, the President's son, chaired the campaign. Lucky me, I had an opportunity to work with history.

The Case, which I had a major hand in writing, was...well, I know how immodest it sounds, but it was darn good.

There were oversize drawings of each level of the ship and the naval architect's rendering of what it would look like. In the Case, I wrote in words that glowed and glistened about how the Yacht would be brought back to pristine and seaworthy condition.

We started calling on folks, the Case in hand. Prospects were under-whelmed. It was Clark Clifford who gave us the clue.

He had been Under-Secretary of State in Roosevelt's administration. We called on him for a gift.

"You folks don't have this right at all. The material is terrible. This program isn't about the restoration of a not-too-pretty boat.

"It's about FDR. It's about an exalted President. But it's really about the Office of the President. It's about the most exciting, dynamic, and fearful period in this nation's history.

"Rewrite that damn thing and then come back and see me."

I felt like a scorned Job, scraping my scabs, penitent and pleading: "Why me, oh Lord— why me?"

Rewrite it we did. The new Case was full of photos of FDR. There were reprints of some newspaper headlines that carried the dateline: *From the Presidential Yacht Potomac.*

We dug into the archives of the FDR Library. There were some treasures. We found photos of many world leaders with the President, taken on the Yacht.

In the new Case, we used no architectural drawings. No display of the proposed renovation. No photos of the Yacht itself. The Case was replete with photos of history.

We couldn't wait to begin showing off the new Case. It is an immense hit. (I'm singing the Doxology.) And it is quite clear donors are giving to the Office of the President and to the memory of FDR— not to the restoration of a boat.

(You'll be pleased to know that Clark Clifford made a leading gift.)

I was reminded of this the other day at Cathy's Coffee Shop. That's where many of our village go on a Saturday morning for gossip and coffee. A friend tells me what happened recently in the third grade of our small school in West Cornwall, Connecticut. That's where I live.

Miss Sheide, the third grade teacher, asked students to supply definitions to a number of words. One of the words given the students was, "salt."

One youngster came up with this interesting thought. "Salt is what you don't notice until someone forgets to put it in."

When I heard the story, I thought— now there's a great lesson here for writers. Our job is to add the salt. The taste. To be the lead scout on the trail to new ideas and programs and to see things others don't yet see.

Your job is to make the Case curiously inviting. You take a cue from what Forrest Gump's mama liked to say: "Life is like a box of chocolates. You never know what you're going to find inside."

"We think too small," said the Chinese leader Mao Tse-Tsung. "Like the frog at the bottom of the well. He thinks the sky is only as big as the top of the well. If he surfaced, he would have an entirely different view."

Your task is to help your readers see the big picture.

"I think we should organize a campaign to raise money for air conditioning. But first we need to write a Case Statement."

17

THINK IN
THE FUTURE

*Someone asked Victor Hugo what pleasure he took in writing
day in and day out, for hours and hours at a time.
"Pleasure?" he said. "I don't understand the question.
I don't take pleasure in it. I do it for the pain!"*

"THAT YOU ARE SITTING before me in this church," the
minister said, "is fact. That I am speaking from this pulpit is
fact. That I believe anyone is listening to me is an act of faith."

I want you to have faith that what I am about to tell you is
gospel. So read carefully.

Age is not important. Not unless you're a cheese, or perhaps a
fine wine.

In most cases, I think it's a mistake to start off with your history.
What prospective investors are more concerned with is: What is
your future?

That's why I suggested earlier you write about your history
toward the end of your document. I called that area of the Case:
WAVING THE FLAG. That's where I usually also include the

mission— unabridged if it is really good, paraphrased if necessary to make it dramatic and understandable.

Putting your history toward the end doesn't diminish your service of the past. If there is a special anniversary or if you have a long existence, it's worthy of noting. But I don't often lead with it. I often do something like this.

We have been serving the homeless in our community for fifty years. Uninterrupted. Around the clock. Every day. And on Thanksgiving and Christmas. Especially on Thanksgiving and Christmas.

We extend hand and heart to all who enter our doors. They find here a loving heart, a hearty meal, a clean and comfortable bed. Counseling when they're ready, chapel if they want it, and work opportunities. And all the coffee they can drink!

We save lives every day. Day in and day out. At any hour. They come to us. They come by the hundreds. Every day. Discouraged, distressed, weak in spirit. And yes, often on drugs. They leave changed. Some are changed forever.

We are proud of our distinguished past. Because of our very special approach, we believe we are one of the premier institutions of our kind in the nation. We have established in this community an extraordinary record of service. We are unrelenting in our commitment and dedication to the homeless and this community.

But it is to the future we look for our greatest achievements. What we envision is beyond anything of the past. That is why this program is so important to you...

You get the idea. It leads quite emphatically into the close. I've tried to wrap the history and mission into describing the value of the projected program.

A Side Bar! I wrote earlier that if you have a special anniversary it is, of course, worthy of mention. I do, however, have a problem tying the fundraising goal to an anniversary. Let's say $25 million for your twenty-fifth anniversary.

It's too perfect. Like a perfect nose, it's unbelievable.

The financial objective needs to be substantiated, carefully documented and validated. It is based on proven and urgent needs, not on a founding. Most important, I have never had a successful campaign based entirely on an anniversary celebration.

Side bar closed.

Now back to the question of including the organization's history. There is an important exception to my rule. If you have a truly distinctive and distinguished history, then certainly it deserves important space in your opening paragraphs.

I'll give you an idea little later of what I have in mind. Just make certain it's a truly significant landmark and is integral to all the organization now does and will do.

Now, I'll give you an example of the worst kind of history.

Our organization was founded in 1887 in Evansville, Indiana, in the old Trinity Lutheran Church on Center and Main Streets. A meeting was held in the sanctuary. Josiah Hockmeyer gathered eleven other kindred Lutherans to talk about the problems of...

Hey, wake up! I think of Dorothy Parker's review of a book: "This writing should not be tossed lightly aside but should be hurled with great force."

You see what I mean. This lesson in history is of interest only to the Hockmeyer family— and probably not all of them. It has all the spontaneity and excitement of drywall. We'll never get the reader past the first paragraph.

When you do use history, you need to show how past performance helps ensure future results. You want your reader to revere the past, and understand your present. But it is to the future where they look for your greatest achievements.

The Roman poet Horace once said that the exceptional writer is one who can wield ordinary words so skillfully that, in his hands, the ordinary is made new.

Your task is to transform your organization's mission and history into a great tomorrow of incalculable service. You are an agent of transformation. You think endlessly in the future tense.

Do you remember earlier I mentioned I would give you an example of when history is important? We managed the campaign for the Hermitage, President Andrew Jackson's home. It is located on a beautiful site outside of Nashville.

It was a working farm in his day. When you visit the Hermitage today, you drive on a narrow road around the property, up a long lane lined with old oak trees. There are cows, and sheep, and horses in the paddock. The sheds, the barns. The structures have been restored, just as they were in Jackson's day.

Quite suddenly, you're back in the 1830s.

Let me take you by the hand for a moment. Notice the tree-covered rolling hills and grass greener than you have ever seen. Spring is the best time of year at the Hermitage. Look at the burst of color. Apple and cherry blossoms everywhere.

Come inside. This is the President's home, precisely as it was when he built it and lived here. He was a popular president and dignitaries from all over the world came to visit him, to this very Sitting Room where you are now.

Walk with me into the parlor. There's Jackson's favorite chair. And sitting next to him is his beloved wife. Did I tell you how he fought a duel and killed a man who made unkind remarks about Rebecca?

And look over there. That grandfather's clock is the very same one that was in that corner when the Jacksons lived here. It belonged to his father.

What I attempted is to get you into the President's home, sitting next to him and Rebecca. That's what we did in the Case.

This is the exception I wrote about earlier. If you have an institution with the kind of history of a Hermitage, you must use it, exploit it, and celebrate it. And of course, you lead the Case with it. But don't make it a history lesson. Take the reader by the hand for a guided tour.

Unless it is truly relevant, history doesn't entice or motivate. The typical reader doesn't have the patience or leisure to go slowly along, step by step, with the writing. Find anecdotes, quotes, action-facts— all of which will reveal the institution.

Here's your charge. Have the reader see your organization's mission and vision through their eyes not yours. Because of your writing, they seek new horizons, break new barriers.

Even the very familiar and mundane take on new prisms and gravity. You are the writer. You make that happen.

Your readers have joined you on a Harrison Ford-like quest for the Holy Grail. They are willing to chart new courses and shape new approaches to new opportunities.

They now understand your proposed program is the only way to effectively serve the future. Your job is to make them see that.

These are confusing and complex times we live in. Unlike anything we have ever known before. These are also the most exciting and opportunity-bursting times in history.

Here's what you know. Growth in your institution will stem from challenging turbulence, not stagnation. If the organization is satisfied, it's dead.

Your charge is to bond the reader to the organization's new and dynamic vision. You take your reader by the hand, from the chaos and confrontations of today's desperate times to a positive response and commitment.

Take a bow. You make it happen.

18

LEAVE NOTHING UNANSWERED

"There are few wild beasts more to be dreaded
than a writer who has nothing to say.
– Jonathan Swift

THERE ARE MANY ELEMENTS that must be included in a Case Statement. That's the mechanical and technical side of developing the material. Writing is the creative side. And nothing takes the place of good writing.

You must prepare copy that empowers and motivates. Material that states clearly and dramatically the need and urgency. Even a project that is unquestionably valid requires writing that has genius, magic, and power.

There's a great deal of difference between brilliance and pizzazz. Cultivate the former in your writing, eschew the latter.

You need to describe in powerful words what there is about your institution that will make the reader commit to a notable gift. What extraordinary element is there about your program that propels your organization to a higher priority in the prospect's giving motivation?

If the reader doesn't share your vision and isn't moved to become a partner in your great cause— no matter how pressing the need, you haven't made the case. Period!

Good writing isn't good enough. It is forever the enemy of being the best you can be. Be an Evangelist for your program. Write with passionate wonder.

John Middleton Murray says that a truly great piece of writing is an exciting tale to the simple, a parable to the wise, and a direct revelation of passionate wonder to the man who has made it part of his being.

No one said it would be easy. There are times your mind is a muddle. Life seems in a state of flux. A blank sheet of paper waits, daring you for an irresistible script.

When I prepare a Case that resonates and really works, I feel a surging sense of achievement. *Quando scripto sento un uccelo, padrony del cielo* (when I write, I feel like a bird, master of the skies.) What Tennessee Williams called, "A great dammed-up emotional ebullience."

Earlier, I gave you eight elements that are fundamental. But don't be unduly concerned about their order in your Case Statement. There are times when it's much more compelling to start with the vision or the urgency. And sometimes, historical facts or details about current services can be handled best as exhibits in an Appendix.

There will be some situations where you combine the elements. Relax. You need not follow a rigid guide. You are a dream merchant. Don't tinker with moments of vision. Write with conviction and zeal and find your own rhythm. It will guide you properly.

What counts is that you leave nothing unanswered or open to challenge. And yes, one thing more— you end up with a Case Statement that represents the Institution with style, grace, and integrity. You want the piece to be a *can't put it down, can't turn it down.*

I've looked for an instrument of some sort for years that would help me assess the writing of some of our staff. And one that helps clients evaluate material they have written.

Does your Case have passion, writing that transforms mission into results? Or does it have the style and dignity of Bob Dole running in his shorts! Or the clatter and clang of emptiness? Or the grace of a hippopotamus dancing on its toes. What Tom Wolfe calls, "Stillborn, ossified, and prematurely senile— avant-garde to the rear."

What was needed is a tool that would help examine and grade a Case Statement. I've never seen such an instrument...so I developed one of my own.

You're going to love it. (Yes, I do show a modest bias.) There is nothing you can add. I use it all the time in testing one of our Case Statements. You will find it in the Appendix.

Oh, sure, I suppose I can be challenged on some of these items but I do feel a bit like Alfred Austin, English Poet Laureate at the turn of the last century, who referred to celestial inspiration in all he did. "I dare not alter anything I do. It all comes to me from above."

Go to the Appendix. Use the *CasE*valuator© to rate the twelve essential factors that determine the effectiveness of a successful Case Statement. Indicate the points for each item in the right hand column. Total the points to score your Case Statement.

19

YOU ARE THE SHEPHERD

"Even if you reject this book, it will have served its purpose— which is to clarify your thinking and feelings. You will at least know what you don't like and are unwilling to accept. And that's a gift of sorts."

– Rita Mae Brown

A LONG TIME AGO, when I graduated from college, I was planning a trip to London. I called a small hotel there to reserve a room for my stay.

I rang.

"Do you want a room with a shower or a bath?" the clerk asked.

"What is the difference?" I assumed the difference was the price.

"Well," said the clerk, "with the bath you sit down."

You can see how easy it is to get things not quite right. Your job is to shed light into the darkness, as the psalmist says. To leave nothing to question.

The shepherd always tries to persuade the sheep that their interests and his own are the same. In writing a Case, you are the shepherd.

Your secret of success is to convey passion in your writing. Unbridled, unflinching, undying passion. Be driven by it. Be an unbiased fool, head over heels, for your institution. Let it burn inside your bones like fire.

Your passion is contagious. Infectious. Your reader feels it. A bonding takes place. You are endlessly inspirational.

What your organization needs is what Stanford Professor James Collins calls a *Big, Hairy, Audacious Goal.* To be the best. To get there first. And make a difference. That's what you want to transmit.

You write with the crystalline depth of an Ansel Adams photograph. You make it come alive. You work in your own way, speak with your own voice, find your own style.

You are the shepherd. Keep that in mind. Your most significant job is to motivate your reader to make an investment in your great cause. You make it irresistible.

You are unambiguous. You are riveted in your focus. Whatever else you cover in your Case, your job is to have the reader live in great anticipation of providing a gift that will make a consequential difference.

When Christ approached a leper, He didn't say: "We haven't been having a great deal of success with leprosy lately. But if you follow my advice, you'll have a so-so chance of survival over the next five years."

"You are healed." That's what He said.

That's how emphatic and unmistakably unequivocal you are with the results that will be achieved.

Keep in mind the six reasons people will give to your organization. Cover them in your Case.

1. They believe in the work of your organization and its unique qualifications to provide the program and services you project.

2. Their gift will change lives or save lives.

3. They want to make a difference.

4. There is philanthropic intent.

5. They are joining others in a worthy cause.

6. You asked them to make an investment.

Your Case must respond to these issues. You do this most effectively by planning in advance.

You're not going to like what comes next. It's an added task you probably hadn't thought about.

You won't like it. But I can't resist touching on the issue— much the same way the tongue uncontrollably seeks the socket of a tooth that's just been pulled. What I suggest makes an extraordinary difference.

Here's what I do before I start the actual writing. It's not what I would like to do most or first. What I really want is to begin the writing. I'm itching to begin. But I know in the end, I'll have a much better Case if I do an analysis.

I make notes. I don't worry about sentence structure, the right words, grammar, or even content. I just begin writing. Here's what I cover:

1. What is the final objective I want to achieve in this Case?

2. What are the kinds of concerns and objections most likely to be raised about the program? About the cost? About the results?

3. What are the most meaningful benefits if the program is funded?

4. Can the results be substantiated?

5. Why is my organization the most effective and the most logical choice for undertaking the program?

6. What are the reasons the reader should make the investment?

Try it. I promise you the results are worth it.

It will cost you a half a day, no more, in preparing it. And it will save you days of writing. It will imbue the Case with life and energy. And it will provide a strategy and structure to your writing.

Here's what I do.

I take a yellow pad and my Mont Blanc pen (smooth as woven Chinese silk). I start writing as fast as possible. I scribble. I use separate sheets for each question. If you prefer 4x6 cards, be my guest. Or, of course, your computer if that's your bent.

You're on your way. The miracle isn't that you will finish the Case. The miracle is that you have the courage to start. It was like diving from the high board.

Keep in mind the Case isn't about needs. Your organization doesn't have *needs*— it has answers. People have *needs*— your organization has the answer. An unparalleled response.

And your Case isn't about money either. It's about changing lives and saving lives. The Case isn't about giving. It's about joining others in a glorious cause that will touch lives in a very special way.

That's why I've saved until last my comments about how to describe the funding of the program. Where do you put that non-inspirational business about the cost, the cold dollars? How much will it cost to fund the dream?

You have written a brilliant Case. The reader is heartened and invigorated (perhaps even inspired) by your every word. You have to talk about the cost somewhere.

I don't like using a long section of figures and dollar signs. Where's the passion in that? It has all of the drama of a diva in decline.

Consider describing the total cost of the program somewhere in the narrative. And using an Appendix to give all of the detail. That way, there will be no interruption in the story.

You have used the theme throughout, and again in the close. You finish with double-thunder to a standing ovation. And the Appendix has all the details and costs.

I am reminded of all you have gone through in preparing the Case Statement. And then, having it approved. No easy task, this. You write of new visions and directions, exciting initiatives, and bright ideas— all with an irrefutable and heightened sense of urgency.

111

I think of the beautiful water lilies in a pond. They represent your finished product. The lilies burst with color and lure.

But hidden beneath the beautiful flowers and leaves are a quagmire of ugly roots and tendrils. And that represents all of the work and travail that has taken place in completing this engaging product.

You have bonded with the reader. Although the Case will be used widely, it gives the feeling it was prepared for only one person. You have motivated the reader to action. To paraphrase Bruce Springsteen— two hearts become one.

20

CODA

*When I first submitted a manuscript to my publisher, some
twenty years and seven books ago, he wrote: "Jerry, I thought
your book was good. They say everyone has a great book
inside him. I look forward to yours."*

ARE YOU LIKE ME? I hate saying goodbye. Do you feel the
same? It's so final. The end.

That's why I didn't call this section: The End, Afterward,
Epilogue, or anything of the sort. "No Epilogue, I pray you,"
Thesus advises in a *Midsummer Night's Dream*.

Coda seems just right somehow: A passage that brings a
movement or a composition to its closing. Notice, *Webster* does not
say— end. With a **Coda**, you know there's more coming.
Sometime.

I thought of this book, in a very modest way, like Tchaikovsky's
1812 *Overture*. Cannons going off, bells clanging, *trantumare*
smashing, *slontrare* soaring, triple-*forte*. A thunderous beginning,
inspiring throughout, and ending at a mountaintop exaltation. The
Coda.

The book wasn't at all that way for you, you say. Well hopefully, here and there, there was some inspiration and direction that will help lead you in your Case Statement. I wanted to draw forth from the music of writing the indispensable bass line over which all our work forms its harmonies.

Every book I write is like a first love for me. I was minding my own business before this book came along. Then I felt the urge. I was in love again.

I feel like Primo Levi. "When the time came, I needed to write this book. I had a pathological need to write it."

I wanted to cover some areas I feel are immensely consequential to our work— the structure of a Case, and how it must propel a reader to action. If it doesn't motivate action, no matter how dazzling the writing— it hasn't achieved its purpose.

Why another book?

I have one life. I want to make it count for something, to make a difference. My faith demands, and this is not optional—my faith demands I do whatever I can, wherever I can, whenever I can, for as long as I can, with whatever I have, to try to make a difference.

There are the last lines in a passage of James Dickey's novel, *To the White Sea.* I feel that way about this book, about writing, and about my profession. As far as this book is concerned, I put myself somewhat in Dickey's words.

"I am in this book, every action, every word of it. I am part of all of it. And I will be everywhere in it from now and for as long as I live. You will be able to hear me, just like you are hearing me now. Everywhere in it, for the first time and the last, even when I close my eyes."

Writing is not my profession. If someone asks me if I am a writer, I would say— I am not. I am a fundraiser who happens to have the urge to scribble. I love to write.

That's why this book, especially, has been a great voyage— the voyage, probably, of my life. I understand Edward Gibbon's comment: "I must acknowledge I have drawn the highest prize possible in the lottery of life."

Some of my neighbors know I write "things." And best of all— they don't hold it against me.

You have read the book and you know how strongly I feel on certain issues. Now do as Sherlock Holmes said to Watson: "You know my methods. Apply them."

The words of the great French writer, Marguerite Duras, resonate. "This book doesn't really end. As it closes, it is just a beginning." **Coda**.

"We've got to develop a strategy of changing our organization's direction without giving the appearance of changing our mission that won't seem to diminish our concern and compassion for those we serve and won't be dismissed as cosmetic and opportunistic, and at the same time, meet all program objectives and give us a positive bottom line that will satisfy the board, make donors passionate about our work, keep the community and our constituencies happy, and tell our story in a dramatic way that will galvanize our prospective givers to our cause.
We'd better call in someone to write a Case Statement."

APPENDIX

SAMPLE THEMELINES

THERE ARE ABOUT 100 THEMES I chose at random from about 1,000 Cases we have written in recent years. Some may be a perfect match for a Statement you're working on.

I discovered something quite interesting. I asked the office to give me about 100 titles. I had never before seen them flat-listed like this. Looking them over in this format, they don't "grab" me the way they did when we developed and reworked them for the actual Statement.

I approve virtually all titles before they are sent to the client for their consideration. At the time, I thought each one was at the very least near-brilliant!

Renaissance by the Riverside (Tampa Museum of Art)

To Grow, To Serve (Salvation Army, Iowa)

The Skill to Heal, The Spirit to Care (Florida Hospital Waterman)

Building the Future, Restoring the Past (Dona Ana Arts Center)

A New Stage for A Grand Old Stage Coach (Stage Coach Players)

Scholarship on Fire! (Baptist Theological Seminary)

Waiting in the Wings (South Bend Civic Theatre)

Lessons for Tomorrow (Allegany College/Bedford Campus)

A Caring Legacy…A Bright Future (Children's Shelter, Texas)

A Burning Issue, A Flame of Hope (Old Firehouse
    Rescue Shelter)

Wilderness in the City (Sand Creek Regional Greenway)

A Building to Treasure, A Treasury of Knowledge
    (Franklin Public Library)

Exceeding Expectations (Scott & White Medical Center)

Some Enchanted Evenings (Center for the Performing Arts)

From Success to Significance (Concordia University)

The Crossroads of Life (Coffeyville Regional Medical Center)

Building on a Dream (West Virginia Public Theatre)

'Something Holy' (Mt. Tabor Center)

Everyone's Favorite Place (West Monmouth County YMCA)

With God's Grace (Los Altos Methodist Church)

An Unmatched Spirit (East Texas Medical/Rusk)

Beyond Measure (Children's Hospital Medical Center)

A Matter of Heart (University Community Hospital)

Close to Our Heart (Good Samaritan Community Healthcare)

A Promise of Renewal (Providence St. Peter Hospital)

Hope for Tomorrow…Today (Salvation Army, Lincoln)

Keeping Faith with the Future (Atlantic General Hospital)

Time to Climb Another Peak (Pikes Peak Region YMCA)

A Place for New Beginnings (Family Services Davidson County)

Setting the Stage for Life (Woodside High School Auditorium)

A Vision and A Reality (North Valley Hospital)

A Tomorrow of Uncommon Promise (Mississippi College)

Part of Your Life (Carson Tahoe Hospital)

One Family at a Time (Birmingham YMCA)

Building on the Best (Mission Hospital)

Welcome Home (Ohio Masonic Home)

Who Will Take Care of Us? (Bryan School of Nursing)

When a House Becomes A Home (FarmHouse Fraternity)

Saving the Last Great Places (The Nature Conservancy)

The Head of Class (Powhatan School)

Setting A New Stage (Lawrence Community Theatre)

A Matter of Life (Carondelet Foundation)

Depend On Us. For Life! (Baptist Medical Center)

How Does Your Garden Grow? (Quail Botanical Gardens)

Keeping A Covenant (Kansas City YMCA)

Keeping Pace with Tomorrow (Baylor Medical Center/Grapevine)

What's In A Namesake? (Lincoln College)

The Right Thing to Do (Queen of the Valley Hospital)

A Lifeline of Hope (The Center for Prevention of Abuse)

We're Here for Life (St. Mary's Hospital)

'Whenever There Is A Need...' (St. Thomas Family Center)

Building on a Promise (Indiana Chapter, Red Cross)

With God's Blessing (Church of the Ascension)

Give A Girl A Future…(Girls Inc. of Greater Santa Barbara)

That Time of Your Life (Munroe Regional Medical Center)

Rekindling A Legacy of Care (Door County Memorial Hospital)

The Campaign for Life (Blodgett Butterworth Health Care
   Foundation)

A Woman's Place (Riverview Hospital)

A Place Where Faith and Healing Meet (Pastoral Care Programs)

Setting the Stage for a Dramatic Future (Toledo Repertoire
   Theatre)

Dream On and Believe (Oklahoma State University)

Beautiful Music. Forever (Evansville Philharmonic Orchestra)

A Path With A Purpose (MeritCare Health Systems)

Making Beautiful Music (South Dakota Symphony)

Discover the River of Dreams (Pocomoke River
   Discovery Center)

A Living Heritage of Humanity (African American
   Cultural Center)

Summa Cum Laude (Notre Dame)

How Do You Top A Miracle (Franklin Road Academy)

Just Imagine! (Children's Museum for Mississippi)

Welcome to Our World (Leesburg Regional Medical Center)

A Promise to Our Community (State College YMCA)

Welcome to Our World (Leesburg Regional medical Center
   OBGYN Center)

The Nature of Tomorrow (Howell Wetlands)

More Than A Hospital (Rice Memorial Hospital)

Tradition Meets the Challenge (Camp Becket/Chimney Corners
   YMCA)

Once In Our Lifetime (Sacred Heart Medical Center)

It's Life That Matters (East Texas Medical Center)

Vision Inspired (Trust for Public)

Making Miracles Every Day (Children's Museum)

Places Never Before Gone (Saint Alphonsus Regional
   Medical Center)

A Covenant with Tomorrow (Scripps Hospital)

GRABBING
THE READER

HERE IS A RANDOM SAMPLING of some opening and closing paragraphs that helped add sparkle and zest to their Case Statements. What you seek are words that grab the reader by the throat and won't let go.

Opening paragraph
At this very moment, an invisible epidemic is sweeping across this country. Last year it claimed 170,000 lives, and the number keeps rising. Right now, it's the fourth leading cause of death by disease in the United States. Nearly sixteen million American's have this disease, and a third of them don't even know it. It isn't cancer. It isn't AIDS, or Alzheimer's. This invisible epidemic is diabetes.
American Diabetes Association

Opening paragraph
The achievements of Roanoke College's last decade owe a great debt to the sacrifice and struggle of all Roanoke generations. It has been a long journey from 1842 to today. But, every new student or tenured professor or brick or book is a step into the future, and an advance toward the victory of significant distinction.
Roanoke College
Roanoke, Virginia

There is little doubt that the new century presents challenging times for higher education, and especially for independent higher education. But with challenge comes opportunity. Since 1870, Wilmington College has combined the practical and liberal arts to help students make a living and make a life. The Wilmington experience continues to have a transforming influence on student's lives.

Our Quaker heritage places peace, nonviolence and social justice at the heart of the College's mission. These values shape what we do and inform who we are.

Wilmington College
Wilmington, Ohio

Opening statement
Students today have more serious interest in spirituality and a deep yearning for meaning beyond materialistic consumption. The faculty of the College takes joy in their personal relationships with students in this Christian environment. It makes an everlasting impact on the lives of students. Our Newberry College is a jewel for the church. This jewel must shine.

Newberry College
Newberry, South Carolina

Opening paragraph
Lakeside School is a place where bright, eager, energetic and motivated students and teachers work together to do amazing things in and out of the classroom. Whether working with DNA samples in the lab, hiking the beaches of the Washington Coast, or playing a LaCrosse match on the field, Lakeside Faculty and students share an enthusiasm and a love of learning.

Lakeside School,
Seattle, Washington

For 150 years, the YMCA has been a pioneering force in the United States— a force so powerful that, as we begin the 21st Century, it is the most successful social institution this country has ever known. Above all, the YMCA is about people— all ages, races, religions and incomes.

YMCA of the USA

Closing paragraph
Students shall find wisdom here and faith. In steel and stone, in character and thought, they shall find beauty, adventure, and moments of high victory.

The University of Pittsburgh
Pittsburgh, Pennsylvania

Opening paragraph
It was a different world when Orange County State College was established on 225 acres of orange groves in 1957. It is an even more dramatically different world today as the College of Business and Economics of California State University, Fullerton looks to a tomorrow that is already here.

Orange County State College
Fullerton, California

Opening paragraph
Be it known by all who enter our doors that Christ is the reason for this school. He is the unseen but ever present teacher in its classes. He is the model of its faculty and the inspiration of its students.

The Summit Country Day School
Cincinnati, Ohio

Opening paragraph
Time does not stand still. Ever. It takes away and marches on. So must a great university. Success breeds confidence. We can not and will not rest on our laurels. There is much more to accomplish.
Oklahoma State University
Oklahoma City, Oklahoma

Closing paragraph
Our mission in values call us to be first and foremost a ministry of healing. We can't be viewed by ourselves or others as just another healthcare business. It's simply not who we are. We are all on a personal journey of faith. While our individual calls are different, there are places along our paths where we can share in faith and support each other. To those who may be considering an opportunity to help in a new or a renewed way, I encourage you to be generous and to tell others about the joy you receive joining with us in our mission.
Saint Thomas Health Services
Nashville, Tennessee

Opening paragraph
The moment has come for Pepperdine to launch into a new era, into the next millennium. Each year our journey will be attended by fresh adventures…our sails have caught the winds of change— and in assurance and anticipation, the voyage begins.
Pepperdine University
Malibu, California

Opening paragraph
If you could invest $100 and get $716 in return, would you? The question is real, because you earn seven times what you give when you invest in the early months and years of a child's life.
United Way of America

Opening paragraph

While higher education experiences a rattling of its moral foundations, Brigham Young University stands firm. It holds fast to its founding commitment to integrate spiritual and secular knowledge. As we press forward with this historic campaign for Brigham Young University, we recognize that BYU has yet to achieve its great potential. It is not yet the fully empowered University we envision it becoming. Achieving such a lofty goal is certainly within our reach, but it will require the continued support of those who believe in the importance of providing the principled, moral education to our youth. Having this support will enable us to persist in the arduous climb up the tower of knowledge that pertains to this earth and its heavens.

Brigham Young University
Provo, Utah

Closing paragraph

But it is our students to whom we have the most urgent responsibility. Although our future will soon be in their hands, their preparation for the future is now in ours. To them we will entrust the reigns of government, the management of our businesses, the education of future generations of our children, and the leadership of our global society.

What they are taught, and how they are taught, is of infinite importance.

. . . the ultimate success of this effort depends on you. Your support will indeed help light the way. Now is the time to increase support of this great school. It is time to press forward, a time to celebrate, a time to shine.

Brigham Young University
Provo, Utah

Opening paragraph
There are no hum-drum days at Highland Hospital. There is nothing commonplace about the work that goes on there. What would be considered exceptional in some other hospitals is the typical and ordinary here. That's the wonder of it all: That within the walls of an aging, inner-city healthcare facility—amazing people are doing heroic things with enormous pride and dedication, to deliver extraordinary care to the sickest and most marginalized people in Alameda County. The stories that unfold at Highland are both brave and brutal, horrendous and heart warming. They bear witness to human tragedy on a huge scale and to human caring on an even grander scale. They carry messages of hope, caring, and commitment.

Highland Hospital,
Alameda County Medical Center
Oakland, California.

Opening paragraph
World Christian Broadcasting invites you to join its band of realistic dreamers, who've learned how to turn an impossible mission into one of history's greatest success stories.

World Christian Broadcasting
Franklin, Tennessee

We welcome the critically ill with hope, and the healthy with a promise of an even brighter future. Once entering the doors, the patient is never, from that day forward, a stranger again.
If we are to defeat the big killers— heart disease and cancer— we must strive for no less than being one of the top medical centers in the country. This requires total commitment. We are prepared and poised. We can provide a Pathway to Life.

New life. Our dream is eradicating cancer and eliminating heart disease. Until we achieve our dream, there is no rest.

Spectrum Health

Grand Rapids, Michigan

Opening paragraph

Extending a hand to forgotten people. Restoring abandoned homes and neighborhoods. Reconciling races. Inspiring leadership. A faith-based approach to doing away with urban desolation. Providing spiritual and economic impact to the inner city. Extending hand and heart through hope.

Fresh Ministries

Jacksonville, Florida

Closing paragraph

We believe in the creation of inspired lives produced by the miracle of hard work. We are not frightened by the challenges of reality, but believe that we can change our conception of this world and our place within it. So we work, plan, build, and dream. We believe that one must earn the right to dream. Our talent, discipline, and integrity will be our contribution to a new world. Because we believe we can take this place, this time, and this people— and make a better place, a better time, and a better people. With God's help, we will either find a way, or make one.

Providence-St. Mel

Chicago, Illinois

Opening paragraph

There's no such thing as a typical day at the Museum of Discovery and Science. There's nothing commonplace about the learning that goes on here. What would be considered exceptions in many schools is simply an ordinary day here. That's the wonder of it all:

That within the walls of a facility that now serves twice the number of people it was built for, dedicated staff members are doing extraordinary things and igniting in all who walk through its doors a newfound curiosity and passion for learning about the world around them.

Museum of Discovery & Science
Ft. Lauderdale, Florida

Opening paragraph
Everyday we are reminded that we are building a university that will last long beyond the days that our individual footsteps mark these paths. Indeed, we are building an institution of higher education that, as with all great universities, is designed to serve not just the moment, but the ages.

Chapman University
Orange, California

Closing paragraph
There is no limit to what a dedicated group of people can accomplish when they are led with respect, joined as a team, and focused on a dream. The Campaign for Change is a revolution. A war. The transformation of a community and the building of better futures for its children. Economic, academic, family and racial barriers to achieving this transformation must come down.

The Urban League
Broward County, Florida

Opening paragraph
At Drew, a historic stone gateway opens onto a University with a vision for tomorrow. A place of innovation and interaction, Drew has prospered over its relatively short history. Small, selective and passionate, Drew is teaching the liberal arts within the context of

today. Given this mission and its superb location, Drew offers students one of the most stimulating environments for learning and research—for discovery – in higher education. Against this background, we have launched a campaign to raise $62 million to build new gateways to and from the world.

Drew University
Madison, New Jersey

Opening paragraph
Approaching its fourth century, Yale University is today one of the world's preeminent centers for instruction, research, and public benefit. Over the years, its scholars have extended the pathways to knowledge. Yale is the guardian of the imagination that both defines and asserts our humanity. The Yale Campaign has few precedents. To succeed, however, Yale must have an unprecedented commitment from those who can best appreciate the University's agenda...Members of the Yale family have always been the trustees of this great treasure.

Closing paragraph
Today this trusteeship falls to a new generation. All who know and love Yale will be called upon to participate with generous enthusiasm in the $1.5 billion program for The Yale Campaign.
Yale University
New Haven, Connecticut

THE *CASE*VALUATOR©

U SE THIS *CASE*VALUATOR© to rate the twelve essential factors that determine the effectiveness of a successful Case Statement. Indicate the points for each item in the right hand column. Total the point to score your Case Statement. Note that the rating of Poor is scored as minus two (-2).

	Poor	Fair	Good	Very Good	Excellent	Points
	-2	4	6	8	10	
1. **Mission Is Stated or Interpreted for Easy Understanding**						
2. **Brief History** *explanation of why institution was founded and societal environment that existed at the time that impelled its creation*						
3. **How Institution Provides Its Services** *indication of constituencies served and statistics, and explanation of activities, programs, and leadership*						
4. **Institution's Vision For The Future** *clearly and dramatically stated*						
5. **Explanation Of The Proposed Project** *description and rational of the items to be covered in the program...and the cost*						
6. **Institution's Singular Role In Meeting The Need** *indication of how institution is uniquely positioned to meet the need through the proposed project*						
7. **Readability Of The Copy**						
Exciting, memorable title						
Compelling section headings						
Theme (title) is woven through material						
Reads easily						
Total *(Page 1)*						

	Poor	Fair	Good	Very Good	Excellent	Points
	-2	4	6	8	10	
Brief declarative sentences—mostly present and future tense						
Short paragraphs						
Strong, inviting opening statement						
Powerful close, a call for action, theme restated						
Emotional and dramatic copy						
8. A Clear Sense Of Urgency *the project must move forward it is one minute 'til midnight, and time will not wait*						
9. Anecdotal Material *numbers and statistics have a place... but dramatic stories provide sizzle and make copy come alive*						
10. Emphasis On Those Who Receive Service *focus is on the need and those served... not on the institution*						
11. Focus On Reader - copy is reader-oriented...how the reader has a stake in the issue...and can help solve the problem						
12. Reader Is Asked to Share In The Vision *invitation is extended to become a partner in the program*						

Total (*This Page*)

Total (*Page 1*)

TOTAL POINTS

Scoring for the *CasEvaluator*©

165 - 200	You have an excellent Case Statement...compelling and urgent...clearly defined. You've made your case! Some fine tuning will make it perfect.
140 - 164	You're well on your way. There is still some work required to make it precisely the case you need...but you don't have much more yet to do.
120 - 139	It's good—but not good enough. You'll need to review all of the items where you scored poorly...and make necessary additions and revisions.
90 - 119	A fair Case Statement won't make the sale...you have major work to do to bring this up to high standards.
89 & Below	Unacceptable...at times, it's easier to start over than to attempt a major overhaul. Don't be discouraged...but your draft can't be used in its present form...you have work to do.

THE FAIL-PROOF CHECKLIST

HERE ARE SOME QUESTIONS you will want to ask, examine, and review before starting your writing. You almost certainly will not use all of this information for your Case Statement— perhaps very little. But it will assure you of an absolute and precise understanding of your organization.

I find that even some who have been at an organization for a long time, perhaps for years, do not have the answers to all these questions.

Don't skimp. Don't skip. Go through the entire roster of questions.

You can have total confidence in this list. Nothing has been forgotten. Use it as a guide to compliment the other areas indicated throughout the book. Check off each question as you complete the material.

√	**How Is The Institution Positioned In The Community And What Is Its Heritage?**
	When was the institution founded?
	What were the circumstances surrounding the beginnings?
	What geographical area does the institution serve?
	Natural resources in the area?
	Industrial and business concentration?
	What distinguishes the area from the rest of the country, state, or nation— a capital, a distribution center, a rural area?
	Describe the population of the service area.
	Population trends. Increasing or decreasing? Aging?
	Level of affluence and occupational types?
	Educational level and cultural types?
	Ethnic origins?
	What are the services offered by the institution?
	How many people use these services? Have they been increased or decreased? Why?
	How much do each of these services cost? Are they furnished free or subsidized?
	What are the services offered by other organizations in the institution's service area?
	Is there any duplication of services or is the organization's niche unique?
	Does the institution cooperate with other organizations in joining programs or use of facilities?
	In the community, is there a need for services not currently being met that the institution could fill if it had increased funds?
	How many potential new users of the institution could you expect to attract if its programs were increased?

√	**Why Is A Fundraising Program Necessary?**
	Why does the institution need funds?
	Is the program for capital or endowment or both?
	Specific components of the campaign and project?
	How will the campaign improve the organization's ability to fulfill its mission?
	How much money does the institution need?
	How will the money be raised?
	Have alternative sources of funding been investigated (government grants, bonds, etc.)?

√	**Is The Institution Fiscally Sound?**
	What is the current operating budget?
	Is the institution operating in the black?
	Who makes the major contribution to the present operating budget?
	Does the institution have a membership drive, annual support campaign, admission fee, or subscriptions?
	Does it have an endowment?
	What are the financial assets and liabilities of the institution?
	Are the fees charged (if any) competitive?
	Does the institution have a Planned Giving program?

√	**Does The Institution Have Strong Leadership?**
	What is the composition of the Board of Directors (or Trustees)?
	How many are on the Board?
	Are different ages and both sexes represented?
	Major business and commercial interests?
	Community minorities or institution's constituency?
	Is the staff well qualified?
	How many persons are on the staff?
	What are the major strengths and accomplishments of the Executive Director and other key staff?
	Does the institution use volunteers and are they effective?
	Do the administrative facilities meet the requirements of the staff and volunteers?

136

ALSO BY
JEROLD PANAS

MEGA GIFTS
Who Gives Them, Who Gets Them

BORN TO RAISE
What Makes A Great Fundraiser; What Makes A Fundraiser Great

FUNDRAISING ALMANAC
(Presently Out of Stock)

BOARDROOM VERITIES
A Celebration of Trusteeship

EXCEL!

FINDERS KEEPERS
Lessons I've Learned About Dynamic Fundraising

WIT, WISDOM & MOXIE
A Compendium of Wrinkles, Strategies, and Admonitions That Really Work

ASKING
A 59-Minute Guide to Everything Board Members,
Volunteers, and Staff Must Know to Secure the Gift

To order any of these books, call (800) 234-7777

INSTITUTIONS PRESS

137

"If you've been looking for help in writing a Case Statement, your search is over. Jerry has a way of inspiring readers."
– Bill Olcott, Former Editor
Fund Raising Management

"Over a twenty-year career in educational administration, including three campaigns, I've collected five books on writing case statements. I have now thrown them all away. Making the Case is the only resource I will ever need."
– Evans P. Whitaker, President
Anderson College

"I recommend reading the book 20 minutes a day, not all in one sitting. Panas stays at a break-neck velocity throughout. Three hours with him is exhausting."
– Fred A. Bleeke, President
Lutheran Foundation of St. Louis

"Reads and is written like a riveting novel— a favorite book you simply can't put down! It had me chomping at the bit to break out of the gate and get to the writing. The book sizzles with excitement, intrigue, and POW."
– John Haberen, President
Rodale Institute

"Jerry's new book is outstanding. I wish it had been available when I started my fundraising career. It's more than a guide for writing the perfect case statement. It places the wit and wisdom of this world-class fundraiser at your disposal."
– David Dunlop, Consultant

"Once I opened the cover, I didn't put it down until I finished the final page. It is passionate, to the point, full of useful information, and very readable."
– Will Rogers, President
The Trust for Public Land

"Jerry Panas is a gifted writer. Each of his books is better than the last one…this is a must book for anyone who writes to penetrate the consciousness of the reader."
– John B. Begley, Chancellor
Lindsey Wilson College

"I found this book to be a little disturbing. First of all, I rarely read a book— I scan, I flip, I thumb. I whistle and think about something I would rather be doing. But here I found myself suddenly reading paragraphs, word for word, and nodding in agreement. It doesn't matter if you have never written a case statement before, or if you are on the firing line daily. There is great material for you in this book."
– Jerry Huntsinger, Consultant and Author

"Every page offers inspiration, encouragement and dynamic tested ideas for writing the case. It's a must."
– Ted Nace
Author and Vice President, Guideposts